BARBECUE America

A PILGRIMAGE IN SEARCH OF
AMERICA'S BEST BARBECUE

Time-Life Books is a division of Time Life Inc.

TIME LIFE INC.
CHAIRMAN and CEO   Jim Nelson
PRESIDENT and COO   Steven L. Janas

TIME-LIFE TRADE PUBLISHING
Vice President and Publisher: Neil Levin
Vice President of Content Development: Jennifer Pearce
Director of New Product Development: Carolyn Clark
Director of Marketing: Inger Forland
Director of Trade Sales: Dana Hobson
Director of Custom Publishing: John Lalor
Director of Special Markets: Robert Lombardi
Director of Design: Kate L. McConnell

BARBECUE AMERICA
Project Editor: Jennie Halfant
Technical Specialist: Monika Lynde
Production Manager: Carolyn Bounds
Quality Assurance: Jim King, Stacy L. Eddy

Pre-Press Services, Time-Life Imaging Center

Printed in the United States
10 9 8 7 6 5 4 3 2 1

TIME-LIFE is a trademark of Time Warner Inc. and affiliated companies.

Library of Congress Cataloging-in-Publication Data

CIP data available upon request:
Librarian, Time-Life Books
2000 Duke Street
Alexandria, Virginia 22314

ISBN 0-7370-1155-6

Books produced by Time-Life Trade Publishing are available at a special bulk
discount for promotional and premium use. Custom adaptations can also be created
to meet your specific marketing goals. Call 1-800-323-5255.

A PILGRIMAGE IN SEARCH OF
AMERICA'S BEST BARBECUE

Rick Browne & Jack Bettridge

TIME
LIFE
BOOKS
Alexandria, Virginia

CONTENTS

Up in Smoke

The Authors' Pilgrimage Across America

I was 42 before I knew true "Q." Rick was two klicks shy of a half-century.

We take no pride in this confession. We simply state it by way of explaining how two otherwise sane working journalists started on a bizarre journey over three years across thousands of heartland miles to the core of America's only indigenous cuisine. Before it started, we didn't know barbecue; we didn't know the crazy, charming, giving, irascible, gifted, hilarious, corny, cunning people who make it happen. Heck, we didn't even know each other.

Then again, we both had deprived childhoods. I grew up in Connecticut, where barbecue was any meat cooked outdoors, especially if you slathered on store-bought sauce before you let the flames char it hard and dry. I don't know what crime this is, but I now know that meat wasn't barbecue. Rick was born in Ontario, Canada, of all places, not exactly a barbecue bastion. His first barbecue was a hamburger scorched black and about as tasty as a hockey puck, which is just what he used it for. He was in Canada, eh?

For me, it all started when, as a senior editor for a travel magazine, I took a trip to Hot Springs, Arkansas, thinking I was going to tour bathhouses. Instead I got waylaid in a place called McClard's Bar-B-Q (505 Albert Pike; 501-624-9586), which I visited because I heard it was one of Bill Clinton's favorite joints while growing up in nearby Hope. Greeted by the smell of hickory fumes, I wandered into the unassuming '40s-style family restaurant, ordered a combination plate and my life changed forever. In no time, I was tearing the meat from ribs and scarfing up mouthfuls of beef and pork that had been slow-smoked over the pit for hours. Where I could, I crammed in spicy beans and pungent coleslaw. Unlike Bill Clinton, I freely admit that I inhaled McClard's smoky offerings.

Then I took a fateful trip west into the land of "Q." Rick Browne, the photographer on the story, came east from the Golden State. Rick and I were assigned to write and produce a story about Kansas City, Missouri (a meat Mecca of revered steakhouses blessed with 75 barbecue restaurants).
We gleefully gnawed, smacked, and salivated our way across the city until someone took a look at my tomato- and molasses-smudged clothes and my

partner's camera bag stuffed with "doggie bags" of ribs and brisket—"for later"—and said: "You know, if you want really good 'Q,' you should go to a contest."

"You're kidding. There are contests? We can eat there?"

"You bet you can, boys."

The next day, we drove across the state line into Kansas for the Great Lenexa Barbecue Cookoff. Our first indication of the size of the smoke-and-spice cult came when we were forced to park a mile from the event and shuttle in with other believers. One was a judge who explained that you learn to pace yourself, taking only a small bite of each or you'd be full in no time. A 10-year-old boy asked to describe the strangest thing he had ever tasted said, "I ate something a couple of years ago, somebody said it might be grizzly bear, but that's supposed to taste like snow tire, and this was better than that."

The night before, 160 contestants had started smoking delicacies that wouldn't be consumed until at least noon that day. They had set up shop around their pits—many homemade contraptions fashioned from oil drums, old industrial washing machines or materials even more bizarre—and smoked cuts of meat in preparation for blind-taste tests by 100 judges. They had tended fires, adding wood chunks here, choking the vent a bit there, adding secret elixirs. Sleeping in shifts, they waited by ember glow in a ritual of checking thermometers, trading grill lies, opening beers and just watching.

This idyllic image lost some of its gravity, however, in the light of day. Jacques Strapp and his Supporters (he's a mortgage banker) were cooking in a freezer converted to a smoker. The Bum Steers cooked a pig in a coffin. A team of IBM execs worked under the banner "I Burnt Mine—Burning the Best Bytes Since 1988." However serious these guys (and ladies) were about their "Q," they were there to have fun.

We were instantly captivated by these legions of dedicated barbecuers who had created a wonderful little culinary subculture oblivious to whichever foreign cuisine had just taken New York by storm or which movie star had teamed with which interior designer and which chef to create some "fabulous space" in Tribeca or Rodeo Drive. For dedicated thousands, this was great American eating and they had built their leisure lives around it. This was their bass boat, their country-club membership, their Porsche all rolled into one. Some of these guys had done sailboats, now they were doing barbecue.

"You know, if you want really good 'Q,' you should go to a contest."

"You're kidding. There are contests? We can eat there?"

"You bet you can, boys."

Co-author and photographer Rick Browne and fellow judge Dorothy Mengering (better known as Dave Letterman's mom) take a break at the Jack Daniel's Invitational.

It was a world of fun. They created names for themselves—"noms de grille," if you will, like the Baron of Barbecue or the Flower of the Flames. They dressed up in costumes and traded stories and told silly jokes. They welcomed strangers in with a "come on in and set a spell; would you like a beer?" charm that was totally engaging to someone who couldn't even get a decent reservation for lunch in my hometown.

But most of all, they had some of the greatest food in the world. We found that out right there in Lenexa. We humbly approached the grill of Karen Putnam, where the decorated cook was giving away meat she had deemed not good enough for competition. Reverently stepping up to the proffered tray of ribs prepared with a "Hollywood cut"—a showman's trick that leaves the most meat possible on either side of the bone—I took communion. I cupped my hands, half expecting her holiness to place the host in them. Instead, I jerked a rib off the tray and into my craw, sucked in a tender mouthful of pork, and nearly sank to my knees.

Hallelujah! The taste of pig and smoke and spice and sauce, all comingling in meat so tender I hardly needed teeth to eat it. I pressed it to the roof of my mouth with my tongue, savoring the complexity of flavor. What was that fruit—raspberry, plum, orange—swimming in the sauce? Were cayenne, paprika, brown sugar, nutmeg peppered in the meat? My eyeballs started floating and I thought to myself: "I'm home at last!"

Rick was off with "The Meatheads" (a.k.a. Ernie and Phyllis Green), a delightful couple who had just won the pork shoulder contest and were celebrating. "Have some butt," Ernie offered. His camera in one hand, a steaming slab of pork shoulder in the other, Rick described the next few moments as the epiphany of his culinary existence. "Suddenly there was a light in the sky, the earth stood still, flavors that I didn't know existed coursed through my mouth—fire and smoke and hickory and oak. I became converted in an instant." He put down the camera and ate with both hands, surely a sign of a future barbecue disciple.

We rushed to buy Smoke & Spice by Cheryl Jamison and Bill Jamison (Harvard Common Press, 1994) and the Kansas City Barbecue Society's own Barbecue…It's Not Just for Breakfast Anymore. Then we returned to our homes in New York and California, where we preached barbecue to anyone who would listen. We were zealots of barbecue. We'd call each other once a week to brag.

But even as we learned to slow-roast at low temperatures for optimum smoke and tenderization, we became scourges of our wives' kitchens. Armed with hundreds of recipes, we'd fill the sinks with dirty dishes. Suddenly we were mixing spices, rubs, powders, marinades, sauces and mops for each meat. Strange new stains marred the counters and floors. The freezer filled up with racks of ribs, pork shoulders and beef briskets. Concoctions with scribbled labels such as "cranberry bourbon sauce" or "hotter than hell rub" littered the place. Utensils were broken, pans burnt, meat thermometers obliterated with soot. Rick bragged about his meat thermometer, which cost him $85, being used in a smoker that cost him $29.

When spring came, we burned to continue our education back in the land of "Q." And then one of us—in retrospect, neither one will take the blame, er, credit—came up with the bright idea that if we did a book about barbecue we could tour all of the shrines of barbecue all in the guise of work. We would write a cookbook—but not just a book of recipes and techniques, but a travel guide to barbecue with photographs that would capture the spirit and humor of America's culinary answer to jazz, an original art form.

Soon we were on pilgrimages to many strange lands: Owensboro, Kentucky; Memphis, Tennessee; Fort Bragg, California; Lynchburg, Tennessee; Arlington, Texas; and Kansas City, Missouri.

As well as enjoying some of the best eats of our lives (both at contests and the roadside stands we insisted on visiting), we learned a thing or two. We learned that barbecuers are some of the friendliest, most generous people in the world. We learned that everybody has his own opinion about what makes good barbecue. And so we learned something about cooking as well, and that is the other purpose of this book: to share the recipes and techniques we picked up from the experts. If you come away from reading this with a smile and the ability to smoke some "Q" that will make your neighbors sit up and take notice, we've done our job.

Jack Bettridge, co-author, casts a skeptical look at a pork entry at the Jack Daniel's Invitational.

Marinades & Rubs

Pork 'n' Brew Marinade

12 ounces dark beer
$\frac{1}{2}$ cup vegetable oil
2 tablespoons wine vinegar
1 teaspoon onion powder
1 teaspoon garlic powder
$\frac{1}{2}$ teaspoon paprika
$\frac{1}{2}$ teaspoon salt
$\frac{1}{2}$ teaspoon ground black pepper

Combine all the ingredients in a saucepan. Simmer for 10 minutes over low heat. Good for beef as well as pork. May also be used as a mop. *Makes about 2 cups.*

Big Game Marinade

2 cups dry red wine
$\frac{1}{4}$ cup balsamic vinegar
$\frac{1}{4}$ cup extra virgin olive oil
6 bay leaves
3 garlic cloves, crushed
1 teaspoon salt
1 shot glass tequila
1 tablespoon lime juice
1 teaspoon dried rosemary leaves

Combine all the ingredients (except the rosemary) in a blender and mix well. Place liquid mix in a bottle, add the rosemary and seal tightly. Put in a cold, dark place for 2 to 3 hours to distribute the flavors. Use within 24 hours on beef steaks, ribs, brisket or roasts, venison, bear or elk steaks. *Makes about $2\frac{1}{2}$ cups.*

Serve with a hearty Merlot, Cabernet Sauvignon or Chianti.

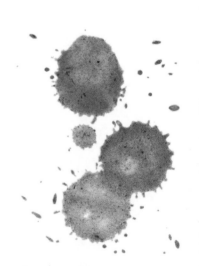

Bird Cookin' Dust

$\frac{1}{4}$ cup salt

3 tablespoons brown sugar

2 tablespoons ground white pepper

1 tablespoon garlic salt

1 tablespoon paprika

1 tablespoon chili powder

1 teaspoon red pepper

1 teaspoon granulated sugar

1 teaspoon onion powder

1 teaspoon ground cumin

1 teaspoon grated lemon zest

Combine all the ingredients. Use on poultry: lightly brush bird with olive oil, then rub spice mixture over and under the skin. Let marinate for up to 12 hours. *Makes about $\frac{3}{4}$ cup.*

Uncle John's Fruit Marinade Spread

1 cup fruity white wine

$\frac{1}{4}$ cup rice wine vinegar

$\frac{1}{4}$ cup extra virgin olive oil

1 mango, seeded

1 small papaya, seeded

2 teaspoons honey

1 teaspoon salt

1 teaspoon ground white pepper

Juice of 1 medium lemon

Combine the ingredients in a blender and mix well. Transfer to a saucepan and cook over low heat until most of the liquid is gone and you have a very moist paste. Use immediately to coat fish, chicken, game hens or duck. Marinate for 3 to 4 hours. Wipe most of the fruit paste off the surface and smoke or grill. *Makes about $3\frac{1}{2}$ cups.*

John Angood, Battle Creek, Michigan
John is married to Kathy, my old English teacher.
John is a superb cook, a talented woodcarver
and a great friend.

WARNING: DO NOT reuse leftover rub or marinade after it has been applied to meat or poultry; it may contain harmful bacteria.

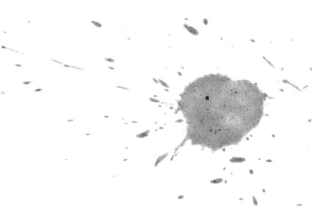

Cuba Libre Marinade

12 ounces cola
1 jigger dark rum
2 scallions, finely chopped
2 tablespoons vegetable oil
Juice of 1 small lime

Combine all the ingredients in a saucepan. Heat on low, being careful not to burn off rum. Cola makes it a very effective and quick (1 to 4 hours) tenderizer. May also be used as a mop. *Makes about $1\frac{3}{4}$ cups.*

Manhattan Marinade

$1\frac{1}{2}$ cups bourbon
$\frac{1}{4}$ cup sweet vermouth
1 tablespoon maraschino cherry juice
1 tablespoon vegetable oil
1 teaspoon onion powder
Dash Angostura bitters

Combine all the ingredients. Shake or stir well. May also be used as a mop. *Makes about $1\frac{3}{4}$ cups.*

Drunken Appul Whiski Marry-nade

2 cups apple juice
1 cup fresh apple cider
1 cup Jack Daniel's sippin' whiskey
1 Golden Delicious or McIntosh
   apple, minced
$\frac{1}{2}$ cup minced sweet onion
$\frac{1}{2}$ cup sugar
1 tablespoon concentrated lemon juice
1 teaspoon Worcestershire sauce
1 teaspoon salt
1 teaspoon ground white pepper
1 generous shot glass Jack Daniel's

Combine all the ingredients (except the last one) in a saucepan and mix well. Simmer over very low heat for 10 to 15 minutes to mix flavors. Put meat in a sealable plastic bag and cover with half of the sauce, reserving the other half to serve at the table. Is heavenly on pork shoulder and ribs, and a delight on shark or swordfish.

Oh yeah. Pour the shot glass of JD into a glass and sip while you cook. *Makes about 5 cups.*

Tee-Many Mar-Toonis Marinade

2 cups gin or vodka
$\frac{1}{2}$ cup dry vermouth (less for dry martini lovers)
$\frac{1}{4}$ cup olive oil
2 teaspoons thyme
2 teaspoons onion powder
2 teaspoons rock salt
Juice of 1 large lemon
1 bay leaf

Combine the ingredients. Shake or stir. Most effective with chicken and fish. May also be used as a mop. *Makes about 3 cups.*

Red-Eyed Meat Marinade

2 cups very strong black coffee
1 large onion, chopped into large pieces
1 cup soy sauce
1 cup dry white wine
$\frac{1}{2}$ cup orange juice
$\frac{1}{2}$ cup molasses
1 teaspoon salt
1 teaspoon ground black pepper

Mix the ingredients in a blender. Place in a Mason jar or ceramic bowl and cover. Use as a marinade on pork butt, rib-eye steaks, prime rib or beef brisket. *Makes about 6 cups.*

Rib Ticklin' Marinade

$\frac{1}{4}$ cup soy sauce
$\frac{1}{4}$ cup vinegar
2 tablespoons sugar
2 tablespoons yellow mustard
2 tablespoons vegetable oil
1 tablespoon ketchup
1 teaspoon cayenne pepper
$\frac{1}{4}$ teaspoon Tabasco sauce

Combine the ingredients in a saucepan. Bring to a boil, and quickly reduce heat to a simmer. Simmer, covered, for 5 minutes. May also be used as a mop. *Makes about 1 cup.*

Soda Jerk

$\frac{1}{4}$ cup onion powder

$\frac{1}{4}$ cup garlic flakes

2 tablespoons baking soda

2 tablespoons freshly ground black and/or
white and red peppercorns

2 teaspoons cayenne pepper

2 teaspoons Jamaican allspice

2 teaspoons ground cinnamon

2 teaspoons ground nutmeg

2 teaspoons brown sugar

1 teaspoon dried sage

1 teaspoon dried thyme

1 teaspoon dried marjoram

$\frac{1}{4}$ teaspoon ground habanero or Scotch
bonnet peppers

Mix the ingredients and place in a jar that can be tightly sealed. Store in the coolest, darkest place in the house. Use with caution, especially if you've used Scotch bonnet peppers. Great for beef, pork or goat dry marinades. *Makes about 1 cup.*

Rick Browne, co-author & photographer
On a trip to the Caribbean for Islands magazine with writer Jim Gullo, we found this Jamaican jerk recipe at a small roadside stand on the way to Kingston. A three-and-a-half-hour journey through hell, the trip resulted in some great pictures, a story about a part of Jamaica tourists seldom see and the hottest rub I've ever tasted.

Sweet Piggie Rubbin' Powder

1 cup packed brown sugar

$\frac{1}{2}$ cup paprika

$\frac{1}{2}$ cup garlic or onion salt

$\frac{1}{2}$ cup seasoned salt

2 tablespoons dry mustard

1 tablespoon celery seed

1 teaspoon ground cloves

$\frac{1}{2}$ teaspoon ground nutmeg

$\frac{1}{2}$ teaspoon ground allspice

1 tablespoon lemonade powder

Combine the ingredients and spread in a dry cast-iron skillet. Air-dry in the sun for 4 to 5 hours, stirring often. If it's damp where you live or you're trying this in winter, set the oven at 200°F. When temperature is reached, turn off the stove. Place pan in oven and leave door ajar while mixture dries for 1 to 2 hours.

To use, rub directly into meat and let stand overnight in the refrigerator. Warm to room temperature and smoke for appropriate time. *Makes about $2\frac{3}{4}$ cups.*

Danny "Bluz Boy" Brodsky, Scotts Valley, California
A great golfer, a great jazz guitarist, a superb barbecuer and a world-class friend.

Sweet-and-Spicy Hickory Rub

1 cup brown sugar
$\frac{1}{2}$ cup hickory salt
$\frac{1}{2}$ cup celery salt
$\frac{1}{2}$ cup paprika
$\frac{1}{2}$ cup ground black pepper
1 tablespoon onion powder
1 tablespoon garlic powder
2 teaspoons cayenne pepper

Mix all the ingredients. Store in a spice container for rubbing on beef and pork. *Makes about 3 cups.*

Chili Con Carnage

$\frac{1}{4}$ cup chili powder
$\frac{1}{4}$ cup paprika
2 tablespoons salt
1 tablespoon oregano
1 teaspoon coriander
1 tablespoon cumin

Mix all the ingredients and use for beef or pork. Store remainder for later use. *Makes about $\frac{3}{4}$ cup.*

Mops, sops and slathers is not the name of a law firm. The words describe different ways of applying sauces and marinades in cooking.

Brisket Rub

$\frac{1}{2}$ cup paprika
2 tablespoons brown sugar
2 tablespoons chili powder
2 tablespoons onion powder
$\frac{1}{4}$ cup yellow mustard

Combine paprika, brown sugar, chili and onion powders and mix. Coat brisket with mustard and sprinkle rub on generously. Store remainder for later use. *Makes about $\frac{3}{4}$ cup.*

Bacon to Basics Rub

$\frac{1}{4}$ cup bacon bits
2 tablespoons paprika
1 tablespoon onion powder
1 tablespoon garlic powder
1 teaspoon chili powder

Crush bacon bits and mix with the rest of the ingredients. Store and use on chicken cuts. *Makes about $\frac{1}{3}$ cup.*

When using thin mops, keep them in handy plastic spray bottles and mist your meat instead of pouring the mop on.

A Tad Tuscan Marinade

¾ cup Italian salad dressing
   (the zestier the better)
2 tablespoons prepared salsa
1 tablespoon sugar

Mix the ingredients in a bowl. Keep refrigera-ed. May also be used as a mop. *Makes 1 scant cup.*

Sweet Tooth Rub

¼ cup brown sugar
¼ cup granulated sugar
¼ cup paprika
1 tablespoon ground ginger
1 tablespoon ground cinnamon
1 tablespoon ground nutmeg
1 tablespoon onion powder
1 tablespoon garlic powder
1 tablespoon salt

Mix the ingredients in a bowl and store for rub-bing on pork or beef cuts. *Makes 1 generous cup.*

Light but Lively Rub

½ cup celery salt
¼ cup paprika
2 tablespoons garlic salt
2 tablespoons onion powder
½ teaspoon ground nutmeg
½ teaspoon ground ginger

Combine the ingredients in a bowl. Store in a spice container for shaking on cuts you don't want too hot, nor too anemic. *Makes 1 cup.*

Hot As Hades Rub

1 cup paprika
¼ cup salt
¼ cup brown sugar
¼ cup crushed red pepper
1 tablespoon garlic powder
1 tablespoon onion powder
1 tablespoon cayenne pepper
1 teaspoon dried basil

Mix the ingredients in a bowl and store in an empty spice container with a sprinkler top. Use for any fur, fish or fowl in need of extra zest. *Makes 2 cups.*

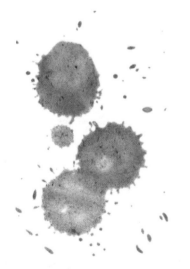

Barbecue Sauces

Heavenly Piglet Barbecue Sauce

2 cups tomato-based barbecue sauce
$\frac{1}{2}$ cup honey
$\frac{1}{4}$ cup molasses
$\frac{1}{4}$ cup packed brown sugar
$\frac{1}{4}$ cup apricot preserves
3 tablespoons cider vinegar
1 teaspoon garlic powder
1 teaspoon coarsely ground black pepper
1 teaspoon ground lemon pepper
1 teaspoon ground red pepper, or season
   to taste
$\frac{1}{4}$ teaspoon powdered hickory smoke

Mix ingredients in a saucepan and cook over low heat for 30 minutes, stirring regularly to blend flavors. Cool and serve, or bottle. Unused sauce can be kept 2 to 3 weeks, if refrigerated. Use as a baste or finishing sauce on pork, chicken or beef. *Makes $3\frac{1}{2}$ cups.*

Angie Morgan Grant, Memphis, Tennessee
Angie's sauce won third place in the tomato sauce category at the 1998 Memphis in May Barbecue Contest.

Lexington Dip

$2\frac{1}{2}$ cups cider vinegar
1 cup ketchup
$\frac{1}{3}$ cup packed brown sugar
$\frac{1}{3}$ cup granulated sugar
1 tablespoon Worcestershire sauce
1 teaspoon onion salt
1 teaspoon freshly ground black pepper
1 teaspoon Kitchen Bouquet
$\frac{1}{2}$ teaspoon dried minced onion
$\frac{1}{4}$ teaspoon crushed red pepper
$\frac{1}{4}$ teaspoon Tabasco sauce

Combine ingredients in a saucepan and bring to a boil, then simmer until sugar dissolves. Cook over low heat for 20 to 25 minutes. Stir in 1 to 2 tablespoons when pulling or chopping pork shoulder, mixing well, then serve the remaining sauce on the side at the table. *Makes about 4 cups.*

Dorothy Lawson Browne, Georgetown, D.C.
My mother, Dorothy Lawson Browne, pulled this out of her family recipe box, saying that she hadn't changed it "much" since it was given to her by her grandmother 80 years ago. "Back then, we didn't have Kitchen Bouquet though," she confesses.

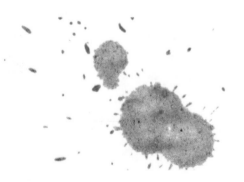

Lone Steer
Brisket Sauce

About $\frac{3}{4}$ pound beef fat, cut from steaks
   or brisket
2 cups ketchup
$\frac{1}{2}$ cup lemon juice
$\frac{1}{2}$ cup lime juice
$\frac{1}{2}$ cup bourbon, beer or water
$\frac{1}{2}$ cup packed brown sugar
1 medium onion, chopped
1 tablespoon Hungarian paprika
1 teaspoon celery salt
$\frac{1}{2}$ teaspoon ground red pepper

Chop fat into large chunks and place in a cast-iron skillet over medium heat until there is 1 cup of fat in pan. Discard unmelted fat and fiber. Add remaining ingredients and cover, simmering for 45 minutes to 1 hour. Bottle or put in a sauceboat to pass at the table. *Makes 3 to 4 cups.*

Bill Payton, Waco, Texas
My roommate in college, Bill was a tall-talkin' Texan who taught me the magic of perfect brisket. This recipe was given to him by a pitmaster at a tiny, greasy, smoky and incredibly popular hole-in-the-wall barbecue joint on the outskirts of Fort Worth.

In 1928, a man came to Alex McClard's tourist court (motel) in Hot Springs, Arkansas, but couldn't pay the $10 room fee. Instead, he turned over a family heirloom barbecue sauce recipe. The rest of the story: McClard used the formula and opened one of the region's and country's most famous and popular barbecue shrines.

Moonlite Black Dip

1 gallon water

2 cups cider vinegar

$1\frac{1}{2}$ cups Worcestershire sauce

$2\frac{1}{2}$ tablespoons lemon juice

$\frac{1}{2}$ cup packed brown sugar

3 tablespoons ground black pepper

2 tablespoons salt

1 teaspoon garlic salt

1 teaspoon ground allspice

1 teaspoon onion powder

Mix ingredients in a large pot and bring to a rolling boil, skimming surface, if necessary. Cook over medium heat for 20 minutes then cool. Use as a baste during cooking and as a dip for mutton, lamb or beef. *Makes about 3 quarts.*

Moonlite Bar-B-Que, Owensboro, Kentucky
This recipe was served for years at Moonlite, one of the best barbecue, family-style eating places in America. Here, lunches are legendary.

PacRim Pourin' Sauce

1 cup Chinese hoisin sauce

$\frac{1}{2}$ cup Japanese rice wine vinegar

$\frac{1}{4}$ cup Taiwanese soy sauce

$\frac{1}{4}$ cup sesame oil

2 tablespoons sake

1 tablespoon honey mustard

1 tablespoon minced garlic

1 teaspoon ground ginger

$\frac{1}{4}$ teaspoon Chinese five-spice powder

Mix ingredients in a saucepan and cook over low heat for 20 minutes. Bottle and let sauce cool. Serve at room temperature. This sauce is especially nice with duck, chicken, game hens or turkey. Or try it on barbecued salmon. *Makes about 2 cups.*

If you want to use a soft drink in a BBQ sauce, don't use diet varieties; they turn bitter when heated.

RB "Q" Sauce

1 cup cola
1 cup tomato sauce
1 can tomato paste
$\frac{1}{2}$ stick ($\frac{1}{4}$ cup) butter (not margarine)
$\frac{1}{2}$ cup Worcestershire sauce
$\frac{1}{2}$ cup packed brown sugar
$\frac{1}{2}$ cup molasses
$\frac{1}{2}$ cup cider vinegar
1 tablespoon maple sugar pepper
1 tablespoon prepared yellow mustard
1 tablespoon chili powder
1 teaspoon summer savory
1 teaspoon onion powder
1 teaspoon garlic salt
$2\frac{1}{2}$ teaspoons balsamic vinegar
1 healthy dash hot sauce or other
    pepper sauce

Mix the ingredients and cook over low heat, partially covered, in a cast-iron pot or skillet until sauce is thick enough to coat the back of a metal spoon. Serve at room temperature on the side with pork shoulder or ribs, brisket, chicken or beef ribs. *Makes about 3 cups.*

Rick Browne, Vancouver, Washington
Having stolen ideas from the best barbecuers around the country, I settled on this Kansas City-style sweet sauce as my favorite. It goes with anything, is a kick to make and can be sweetened, spiced up or toned down as your taste buds desire. Experiment, have fun with this, empty the cupboards and spice rack. After all, barbecue isn't cordon bleu cooking, it's only barbecue!

The Diddy-Wa-Diddy sauce contest, part of the American Royal Barbecue Contest, was started by Remus Powers (whose real name is Ardie Davis) in 1983 and today is the largest of its kind in the world. A panel of more than 100 judges tastes and rates more than 400 barbecue sauces and 100 dry-rub formulas each year.

Sunrise BBQ Sauce

1 cup white vinegar
$\frac{3}{4}$ cup yellow mustard
$\frac{1}{2}$ cup water
1 small yellow onion, minced
$\frac{1}{4}$ cup puréed tomatoes
2 tablespoons minced garlic
$2\frac{1}{2}$ teaspoons Hungarian paprika
$1\frac{1}{4}$ teaspoons salt
$\frac{1}{2}$ teaspoon ground white pepper
$\frac{1}{4}$ teaspoon ground red pepper

Mix ingredients in a saucepan and simmer over low heat for 30 minutes, stirring regularly to blend flavors. Cook until the onions are very tender and liquid has reduced by half. Cool and serve. Unused sauce can be kept for 2 to 3 weeks, if refrigerated. Use as a baste or finishing sauce on pork, chicken or beef. *Makes about* $1\frac{1}{2}$ *cups.*

This sauce is loosely based on the superb sauce served at Maurice's Piggie Park, in West Columbia, South Carolina. Or you can buy the sauce by calling 1-800-MAURICE and ordering a bottle.

For a tasty and spicy treat: Place one or two habanero or chili peppers in a jar of honey for 2 to 3 weeks. Remove the peppers and you have a spicy condiment to use in barbecue sauces or marinades.

Fractured Béarnaise Sauce

1 large shallot, minced
$\frac{1}{2}$ teaspoon dried tarragon
$\frac{1}{2}$ teaspoon dried basil
2 tablespoons vegetable oil
$\frac{1}{4}$ cup tarragon vinegar
$\frac{1}{4}$ cup cooking sherry
2 tablespoons tomato paste
1 stick ($\frac{1}{2}$ cup) butter
3 egg yolks
$1\frac{1}{2}$ tablespoons lemon juice
Salt
Ground white pepper

Sauté shallot, tarragon and basil in oil in a small saucepan. Add vinegar, sherry and tomato paste. Boil to a paste. Melt half the butter and keep liquid at the ready. Cut remaining butter into tablespoons. Whisk egg yolks and beat into a double boiler, turning constantly over hot water. When eggs are smooth and fluffy, but not scrambled, remove immediately and whisk in cold butter 1 tablespoon at a time. When smooth again, drip in melted butter and lemon juice, whisking continuously. Salt and pepper to taste. Use on grilled beef or poultry. *Makes about 1 cup.*

Our friends all think Béarnaise sauce is too highfalutin for barbecue, so we created this tomato-mixed concoction to put them off the trail, while we enjoy our steaks.

There is a certain barbecue establishment on the outskirts of Nashville that plays a dirty trick on its restaurant competitor across the road. During lunchtime, when cars pull into the lot across from his barbecue pits, the pitmaster pours pork grease on an open bed of coals in front of his restaurant. The resulting pungent, mouth-watering clouds of smoke drift across the street, enveloping the customers of this nationally known fast-food eatery in olfactory heaven. They often locate the source of the tantalizing smoke, hop right back into their cars, drive across the street and chow down on superb barbecue pork shoulder, brisket and chicken.

Old English Sauce

6 ounces pale ale
$\frac{1}{2}$ cup tomato-and-molasses-based barbecue
   sauce
2 tablespoons prepared horseradish
2 tablespoons English mustard
1 tablespoon onion powder
$\frac{1}{4}$ teaspoon ground black pepper

Mix ingredients and use on roast beef. *Makes about $1\frac{1}{2}$ cups.*

Plum Good Sauce

$\frac{1}{4}$ cup packed brown sugar
1 tablespoon ground white pepper
1 tablespoon prepared yellow mustard
1 teaspoon ground cinnamon
1 tablespoon vegetable oil
1 cup ketchup
$\frac{1}{2}$ cup vinegar
$\frac{1}{2}$ cup plum butter
2 tablespoons molasses

Sauté sugar, pepper, mustard and cinnamon in oil. Add ketchup, vinegar, plum butter and molasses, stirring vigorously. Simmer for 30 minutes. Use on game, duck or pork. *Makes about $1\frac{3}{4}$ cups.*

Barbecued meat should "rest" in aluminum foil for at least 20 minutes after taking it off the grill. This lets the juices retreat into the meat and makes it easier to carve.

Pork

BBQ'ed Pork Ribs

1 2-pound slab of pork ribs
1 cup cider vinegar
1 cup white wine
$\frac{1}{4}$ cup balsamic vinegar

Marinate ribs in half of the vinegar-wine mixture overnight in a covered dish in the refrigerator. Place remaining marinade in a plastic spray bottle. Remove ribs and let meat rest until it reaches room temperature. When smoker is up to temperature (220°F to 240°F), place meat in rib rack on grill. Cook for 5 to 6 hours, moistening once an hour with spray bottle of marinade. The ribs are ready when they are fork-tender and have an internal temperature of 180°F.

Serve with your favorite barbecue sauce on the side. *Serves* 4.

In colonial Williamsburg, the Labor Day weekend is celebrated by cooking a whole hog the way 18th-century pitmasters did: basting the hog generously with a mixture of saltwater and melted butter.

Big ol' Whole Hawg

1 dressed whole hog (130 to 150 pounds)
1 large apple or orange
1 quart extra virgin olive oil
2 cups paprika
1 cup freshly ground black pepper
1$\frac{1}{2}$ cups garlic salt
$\frac{1}{2}$ cup chili powder
$\frac{1}{2}$ cup dried summer savory
$\frac{1}{2}$ cup dried oregano
$\frac{1}{2}$ cup onion powder
3 tablespoons ground red pepper

Basting sauce:
1 gallon apple juice
1 gallon cider vinegar
1 pound butter, melted

Trim excess fat from body of dressed hog. Cover snout, tail and ears with aluminum foil and hold in place with toothpicks. Insert large apple or orange into hog's mouth. Rub olive oil into flesh and then work mixed dry spices into flesh. Place hog on smoker, skin side down, rear end toward heat source and cook at 270°F for 4$\frac{1}{2}$ hours. Damper fire so heat reduces to 230°F to 240°F. Baste well with sauce and fill cavity with half the remaining sauce; baste every 2 hours for 10 to 12 hours. After 7 hours, turn hog so head is toward heat source. Hog is ready when internal temperature is 170°F. Before serving replace apple or orange with fresh fruit. *Serves* 40-50.

Barbecued Bologna

1 medium onion, chopped
2 tablespoons butter
1 cup tomato sauce
$\frac{1}{4}$ cup clam broth
1 tablespoon dried parsley
$\frac{1}{2}$ teaspoon garlic powder
1 2-pound tube of bologna

Sauté onion in butter. Add tomato sauce, clam broth, parsley and garlic powder. Cook for 5 minutes on low heat. Score bologna to $\frac{1}{8}$ inch throughout. Pour on sauce and let sit for 25 minutes. Bring grill to 250°F. Cook for 90 minutes or until bologna is warm throughout and sauce becomes crusty. *Serves* 4-6.

Smokin' Dogs

Lest we forget as we get so caught up in our rarefied barbecue roots, here's one for the minimalists. Sometimes a barbecue is little more than a cookout.

Plump pork hot dogs
Yellow mustard
Tomato-based barbecue sauce
Grated cheddar cheese (optional)
New England-style frank rolls

Score hot dogs slightly. Place on smoking grill at 300°F. Cook for about 30 minutes. Mix mustard and barbecue sauce as relish. If you're not a purist, slice dogs lengthwise 5 minutes before removing from grill and stuff with cheese.

Country-Style Ribs

4 pounds country-style pork ribs
12 ounces cola
1 jigger dark rum
Juice of 1 small lime
2 scallions, finely chopped
2 tablespoons vegetable oil
2 tablespoons ground mustard
2 tablespoons paprika
2 teaspoons pepper

Country-style ribs (from the blade end of the loin) are the pig's meatiest part, but take some boiling to soften them for the grill. Here is one way to do it:

Cover ribs in a large pot with water. Bring to a boil and simmer 30 minutes. Combine cola, rum, lime, scallions and oil in a saucepan. Heat on low, being careful not to burn off the rum. Use on ribs as a marinade and refrigerate for 2 hours. Mix mustard, paprika and pepper and coat ribs. Grill over medium heat until crisp. Mop often. Serve with a tomato-based sauce. *Serves 4-6.*

Pork spareribs come from the belly of the hog, next to the bacon. They are superb on the barbecue grill because the combination of fat and pork works wonders when slowly smoked.

Quick Butt

$\frac{1}{4}$ cup packed brown sugar
$\frac{1}{4}$ cup granulated sugar
$\frac{1}{4}$ cup paprika
1 tablespoon ground ginger
1 tablespoon ground cinnamon
1 tablespoon ground nutmeg
1 tablespoon onion powder
1 tablespoon garlic powder
1 tablespoon salt
$\frac{1}{2}$ pork butt ($2\frac{1}{2}$ to 3 pounds)
12 ounces cola
1 jigger dark rum
2 scallions, finely chopped
2 tablespoons vegetable oil
Juice of 1 small lime

Two hours before you plan to cook, mix sugars, spices, onion and garlic powders, and salt and rub thoroughly on pork butt. Reserve remaining rub. Refrigerate 1 hour. Mix cola, rum, scallions, oil and lime juice. Pour over pork butt and let stand 1 hour at room temperature, turning several times. Reserve liquid for mop. Prepare grill at 300°F. Cook 2 to 4 hours or until internal temperature reaches 180°F, basting often. Let stand at room temperature for 15 minutes and shred pork for sandwiches. *Serves* 4.

Girded Loins

2 teaspoons ground ginger
1 teaspoon white pepper
$\frac{1}{4}$ teaspoon garlic salt
$\frac{1}{4}$ teaspoon ground cloves
1 3- to 4-pound boneless pork loin

Meat baste:
$\frac{1}{4}$ cup palm or brown sugar
$\frac{1}{4}$ cup soy sauce
$\frac{1}{4}$ cup pineapple juice

Rub spice mixture into meat and marinate for 4 to 6 hours. Place pork loin, fat side up, on grill away from heat. Baste often with sugar-soy-pineapple mixture during cooking time of 2 to $2\frac{1}{2}$ hours. When internal temperature reaches 170°F, place meat in foil and seal tightly. Keep warm until ready to serve. *Serves* 4-6.

Katie's Best Butt

5 tablespoons brown sugar

2 tablespoons paprika

1 tablespoon maple pepper

1 tablespoon lemon pepper

1 tablespoon chili powder

1 tablespoon dried summer savory

2 teaspoons granulated garlic

2 teaspoons seasoned salt

1 teaspoon onion powder

$\frac{1}{4}$ teaspoon crushed red pepper

$\frac{1}{4}$ teaspoon ground cloves

$\frac{1}{4}$ teaspoon ground nutmeg

1 5- to 6-pound pork butt, trimmed

3 cups apple juice

$\frac{1}{2}$ cup apple brandy

Mix all the dry ingredients and rub into the trimmed pork butt. Cover and marinate in the refrigerator overnight, if possible. If not, wait at least 1 hour before cooking. Let meat sit at room temperature for at least 30 minutes before cooking.

Place pork on smoker grill rack over water pan. In water pan you can add sliced apples and oranges for a nice fruity steam. Smoke the meat with lid down over medium coals, turning every hour, for 6 to 8 hours or until bone wiggles easily when pushed. Baste with apple juice and apple brandy mixture after 3 hours at 1-hour intervals when you turn meat. Let meat sit covered for 20 to 30 minutes. Slice, pull or chop meat and serve. *Serves 6-8.*

Katie Welch, Hartford, Connecticut
This recipe was passed down to Katie from her mother, Theresa, who learned to cook barbecue from her grandmother, who emigrated from Hungary to Nashville, Tennessee, in 1905.

Memphis Dry Ribs

2 3-pound (or less) pork rib slabs

Rib rub:
$\frac{1}{2}$ cup paprika
$\frac{1}{2}$ cup garlic salt
$\frac{1}{2}$ cup brown sugar
$\frac{1}{4}$ cup ground black pepper
2 tablespoons chili powder
1 tablespoon dried oregano

Basting spray:
$\frac{1}{2}$ cup olive oil
$\frac{1}{2}$ cup beer
$\frac{1}{4}$ cup lemon juice
1 tablespoon steak sauce

Mix rub ingredients. Use two-thirds of the mixture to rub into ribs. Place in covered pan and refrigerate overnight. Let ribs warm to room temperature and place in smoker (temperature 210°F to 230°F) for 5 to 6 hours, turning once an hour and moistening with basting spray each time you turn them. Take ribs off heat and, after spraying again, sprinkle with the remaining one-third of dry spice mix. Cover tightly in foil and let rest for 20 minutes before serving.

Ribs are perfect served like this, but if your guests prefer, you can serve a favorite barbecue sauce on the side. *Serves* 4-6.

North Carolina Pork Shoulder

1 14- to 16-pound pork shoulder

Dry marinade:
$\frac{1}{2}$ cup brown sugar
$\frac{1}{4}$ cup paprika
$\frac{1}{4}$ cup garlic salt
2 tablespoons ground black pepper
2 tablespoons onion powder
2 tablespoons chili powder
1 tablespoon ground sage
1 teaspoon dry mustard
$\frac{1}{2}$ teaspoon cayenne pepper
$\frac{1}{2}$ teaspoon dried thyme

Have butcher trim fat from shoulder, leaving a 4-inch portion of fat at the shank (bone) end. Rub well with dry marinade (saving a handful for later), working into every inch of the shoulder. Put in a large plastic bag or bowl and cover. Refrigerate for 24 hours. Bring to room temperature and place on cooker, which has been preheated to 220°F. Cook for 11 to 13 hours or until internal temperature is 180°F.

Remove meat from smoker and cool to 140°F. Pull meat from bones and either shred it or chop it and place in a large bowl or glass container. Sprinkle meat with the remaining handful of mixed spices and mix well. Place in foil pouch and seal completely. Serve with buns, coleslaw, pickles, sliced onions and North Carolina-style vinegar-pepper-sugar barbecue sauce. *Serves* 10-12.

Pickin' Picnic

12 ounces dark beer
$\frac{1}{2}$ cup vegetable oil
2 tablespoons wine vinegar
1 teaspoon onion powder
1 teaspoon garlic powder
$\frac{1}{2}$ teaspoon paprika
$\frac{1}{2}$ teaspoon salt
$\frac{1}{2}$ teaspoon black pepper
1 6-pound pork shoulder
1 tablespoon cayenne pepper
1 tablespoon dry mustard
2 tablespoons sugar

The night before you cook, combine beer, oil, vinegar, onion powder, garlic powder, paprika, salt and pepper in a saucepan. Heat for 10 minutes at a simmer. Place pork in resulting marinade and refrigerate overnight, turning several times. In the morning, reserve marinade as mop and rub down pork with cayenne, mustard and sugar. Return pork to the refrigerator for at least 4 hours. Prepare grill to 300°F and smoke pork, mopping liberally. Cook for 2 to 4 hours or until meat reaches internal temperature of 170°F. Set out for 30 minutes and shred meat. Serve in sandwiches. *Serves* 6-8.

Pork Chops

¾ cup Italian salad dressing (the zestier the better)
2 heaping tablespoons applesauce
2 tablespoons prepared salsa
1 tablespoon sugar
Salt and pepper to taste
6 pork chops, 1 inch thick, trimmed

Mix salad dressing, applesauce, salsa, sugar, salt and pepper at least 4 hours before cooking. Thoroughly slather chops with marinade in shallow nonreactive pan. Cover and refrigerate. Reserve excess for mopping. Prepare grill. Smoke chops for 1 hour or until meat thermometer placed in the center reads 160°F. Mop occasionally with remaining marinade. *Serves* 4-6.

The Swine Flew BBQ team cooks in a converted Cessna equipped with a "meat-seeking" missile.

Some o' Dem Chops

6 pork chops, about 2 inches thick

Marinade:

2 cups apple cider

$\frac{1}{4}$ cup fresh orange juice

$\frac{1}{4}$ cup brandy

$\frac{1}{4}$ cup garlic salt

1 tablespoon ground white pepper

$\frac{1}{4}$ cup packed brown sugar

1 tablespoon chili paprika

1 tablespoon dried sage

Place chops and the marinade ingredients in a sealable plastic bag and refrigerate for 4 to 6 hours. Remove chops and reserve liquid. Bring to room temperature. Grill over medium coals until cooked through, turning and basting often with reserved liquid. *Serves 6.*

In South Carolina, a "Truth in Barbecue" law makes restaurants put up notices letting customers know if they cook with wood or other fuels and if they cook whole hogs or just part of the hog.

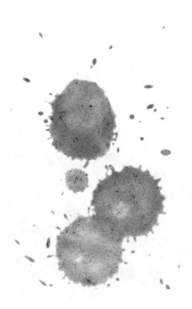

Barbecued Baby Backs

4 baby back rib racks, about
   2 pounds each
2 tablespoons paprika
2 tablespoons seasoned salt
2 teaspoons garlic powder
2 teaspoons onion powder
1 cup beer
1 cup apple juice

Trim membrane from rib racks. Mix paprika, salt, garlic powder and onion powder. Rub liberally into ribs. Wrap in aluminum foil and place in refrigerator for 4 hours. Prepare smoker to 250°F to 275°F. Place ribs in foil on grill for 2 hours. Remove foil and place ribs on grill for 1 hour away from flame, spraying liberally with beer and apple juice mixture. Coat with favorite sauce and cook for 30 minutes, being vigilant not to let sauce create hard coating.

Baby back ribs (from the center of the loin) are the most delicate the pig has to offer and some care should be used not to cook them too hard and crisp. *Serves 4-6.*

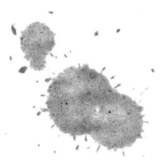

Poultry

Beer Butt Bird

1 4- to 5-pound chicken

Dry rub:
1 teaspoon palm sugar
1 teaspoon garlic powder
1 teaspoon onion powder
1 teaspoon cayenne pepper
1 teaspoon paprika
1 teaspoon dry yellow mustard
1 tablespoon finely ground sea salt

Basting spray:
1 cup apple cider
1 tablespoon balsamic vinegar

Steaming liquid:
12 ounces of your favorite beer
(canned fruit juice can be substituted)

When cooking big birds, wrap the parts in aluminum foil at different intervals (wings first, then legs, then breast) to maximize the smoke time on bigger pieces, which can take the heat.

Wash, dry and season chicken generously inside and out with rub. Work mixture well into skin and under skin wherever possible. Set aside, covered, at room temperature for an hour or so. Drink half the can of beer. Place can on smoker grill and lower chicken onto can so that the legs and can itself hold the chicken upright. This positioning does two things: First, it helps drain off fat as the chicken cooks; second, the beer steams the inside of the chicken, making it the most moist bird you've ever laid yer eyes on.

Smoke 2 to 21 hours, spraying with basting spray several times, until chicken is done and internal temperature is 180°F for a whole chicken. Carefully remove the bird still perched on the can and place on serving tray. After your guests have reacted appropriately, remove the chicken from can (careful! that aluminum can is very hot, use oven mitts) and carve. *Serves 4-6.*

Dat Ded Bird Thang

1 large chicken (5 pounds or more), butterflied

Dry rub:

1 teaspoon paprika

1 teaspoon dried basil

1 teaspoon seasoned salt

$\frac{1}{2}$ teaspoon maple pepper

$\frac{1}{2}$ teaspoon ground thyme

$\frac{1}{2}$ teaspoon chili powder

$\frac{1}{4}$ teaspoon onion salt

$\frac{1}{4}$ teaspoon cayenne pepper

Baste:

1 cup pineapple juice

$\frac{1}{2}$ cup bourbon or whiskey

$\frac{1}{2}$ cup packed brown sugar

$\frac{1}{4}$ cup concentrated lemon juice

$\frac{1}{4}$ cup steak sauce

$\frac{1}{2}$ cup melted butter

Wash and pat-dry chicken. Rub both sides of butterflied chicken with dry rub and let sit in covered glass baking dish in the refrigerator for up to 8 hours. Before cooking, brush off excess rub, then place in water smoker, skin side up, and brush with baste. (For a more flavorful smoke, mix apple, cherry, peach or pear wood with oak for smoke.) Cook at 200°F for $3\frac{1}{2}$ hours, moistening with basting mix every half hour. When done, wrap in foil, pour in remaining baste and seal tightly, setting on counter to seal in juices and absorb sauce. Cut chicken into quarters using poultry shears and serve. *Serves 4-6.*

Apple & Onion Smoked Turkey

1 12- to 14-pound turkey

Dry rub:
$\frac{1}{2}$ teaspoon oregano
$\frac{1}{2}$ teaspoon ground sage
$\frac{1}{4}$ teaspoon garlic powder
$\frac{1}{4}$ teaspoon salt
$\frac{1}{4}$ teaspoon freshly ground black pepper
$\frac{1}{4}$ teaspoon ground celery seed
$\frac{1}{4}$ teaspoon poultry seasoning

Stuffing spices/fruit:
1 lemon, cut into quarters
1 apple, cut into quarters
1 orange, cut into quarters
1 onion, cut into quarters
1 bunch fresh rosemary (5 or 6 sprigs)

Basting spray:
$\frac{1}{2}$ cup apple juice
$\frac{1}{2}$ cup white wine

It takes approximately 24 hours to thaw a frozen five-pound chicken in a refrigerator.

Rinse turkey. Remove giblets. Pat-dry. Sprinkle inside of cavity with dry rub. Place quartered fruit and onion and rosemary sprigs inside turkey. Close opening with a dry French roll or thick slice of bread.

Place bird over water pan in smoker. Cook for 4 to 41 hours, moistening two or three times during cooking time with basting spray. Use white oak, apple and alder wood (if available). Don't oversmoke; a little bit of smoke over a 4-hour period adds up to a heap o' smoke.

If it's Sunday and you're watching a pro game, don't even look at the turkey until the second half begins. If you're enjoying a baseball game, take the first peek at the seventh-inning stretch. When the internal temperature of the thigh (or thickest part of the bird) reaches 160°F seal bird in foil after final and generous spray of baste liquid. Take off heat and let the turkey rest and reabsorb its juices for 20 to 30 minutes. Have a sip o' cider or a brew and sharpen that carvin' knife. *Serves* 10-12.

Really Wild Turkey

2 cups Wild Turkey bourbon
  (or substitute your favorite hootch)
2 cups whole milk
2 cups orange juice
$\frac{1}{4}$ cup corn oil
$\frac{1}{2}$ teaspoon cayenne pepper
1 10- to 12-pound turkey
1 tablespoon paprika

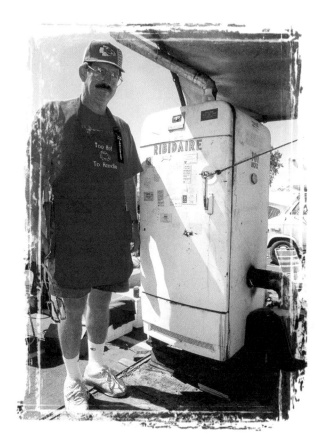

The night before you plan to cook, mix bourbon, milk, orange juice, corn oil and cayenne pepper. Remove giblets from the turkey. If you have a kitchen syringe, inject liquid into the turkey in several places and use remainder as marinade. Otherwise simply store the turkey in a plastic bag with the marinade and refrigerate, turning several times. One hour before cooking, remove the turkey from refrigerator and rub down with paprika. Let sit at room temperature. Prepare the smoker for barbecuing at 300°F. Cook 4 to 6 hours or until internal temperature reaches 170°F. Let sit for 30 minutes before carving (bird should continue to cook to 180°F). *Serves 8-10.*

This recipe was inspired while watching a TV chef cook turkey with brandy on television. We figured such an American dish deserved a more local libation.

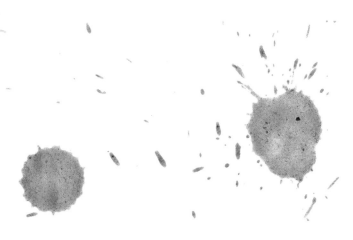

Gobbler Burgers

2 pounds ground turkey
1 medium onion, finely chopped
Paprika
Ground black pepper
Garlic powder
Chopped cilantro
Apple juice

Two hours before cooking, combine turkey and chopped onion in a bowl. Form into 8 patties. Sprinkle with paprika, black pepper, garlic powder, and cilantro to taste. Bring smoker to 250°F. Place burgers on grill away from flame. Cook 1 hour, occasionally spraying with apple juice. Because of health considerations, burgers should be well cooked. Serve on buns with mustard and ketchup or sauce of choice. *Serves 4-6.*

Rich Davis of Kansas City, founder of the KC Masterpiece restaurant chain, reportedly plants two trees for every one used in the restaurants' barbecue pits.

Chicken Fajita-ville

1 tablespoon paprika
2 teaspoons black pepper
1 teaspoon sugar
4 large chicken breasts
2 large green peppers
2 large red peppers
4 large onions
2 tablespoons extra virgin olive oil
8 large tortillas

Mix paprika, pepper and sugar and rub thoroughly into chicken. Refrigerate 3 hours. Slice peppers and onions. Prepare fire (preferably with mesquite) at 250°F. Lay chicken and vegetables on grill, with vegetables as far away from fire as possible. After 30 minutes, turn chicken and remove vegetables. Sauté vegetables in a frying pan in oil until soft. Warm tortillas in oven in aluminum foil. After 30 minutes, remove chicken. Dice chicken and peppers. Chop onions. Serve on tortillas with rice, beans, guacamole and salsa. *Serves 4.*

Split (Personality) Chicken

1 4- to 5-pound chicken, cut into pieces
Shortening, for frying

Marinade:
4 cups buttermilk
2 tablespoons Jamaican Pickapeppa Sauce

Frying coat:
$1\frac{1}{3}$ cups flour
2 tablespoons bacon bits
$\frac{1}{2}$ teaspoon paprika
$\frac{1}{4}$ teaspoon onion salt
$\frac{1}{4}$ teaspoon freshly ground black pepper

Garnish:
2 tablespoons bacon bits
2 tablespoons dried parsley

Wash and pat-dry chicken. Put chicken in a large plastic bag and cover with half the buttermilk-pepper sauce mixture, reserving the other half in another container. Place in a pan in the refrigerator and chill overnight, turning once or twice. Just before cooking, remove chicken and let stand at room temperature for 30 minutes.

Drain chicken pieces (discard liquid) and cook on smoker grill for 30 to 40 minutes at 220°F over oak-hickory or fruitwood smoke. Remove partially cooked chicken and, using remaining marinade, soak for 15 to 20 minutes in a flat pan.

Put flour, bacon bits, paprika, onion salt and pepper in a large bag. Drain buttermilk from chicken pieces and drop them one at a time into the bag, shaking and coating each piece with flour mixture.

Melt shortening in a large skillet and heat until fat bubbles. Fill pan with chicken pieces, placing pieces skin side down. Cover, reduce heat to medium and fry each side for 10 minutes.

Drain and place chicken on paper towels, then place on heated platter. Sprinkle bacon bits and dried parsley over chicken just before it's served. Crispy and crunchy outside, smoky moist inside. Wowser!!! *Serves 4-6.*

Honey Dijon
Barbecued Chicken

1 3-pound chicken, cut into quarters
$\frac{1}{2}$ cup olive oil
$\frac{1}{2}$ cup white zinfandel
$\frac{1}{4}$ cup clover honey
2 tablespoons Dijon mustard
2 garlic cloves, crushed
1 teaspoon ground black pepper
$\frac{1}{2}$ teaspoon salt

Wash and pat-dry chicken and place in two sealable plastic bags. Pour mixture of oil, wine, honey, mustard, garlic, pepper and salt over chicken. Seal. Marinate in refrigerator for 2 to 4 hours, turning occasionally.

Place remaining marinade in a saucepan and heat to boiling, then let simmer for 5 minutes.

Grill chicken with lid down over medium-hot coals for 20 to 30 minutes per side or until cooked through, basting frequently with the reserved marinade. *Serves* 4.

Carolyn Wells, co-founder,
Kansas City Barbecue Society

Harvey Duckbanger

¾ cup vodka
¼ cup orange juice
2 tablespoons Galliano
1 5-pound duckling
1 teaspoon garlic powder
Cayenne pepper

Mix vodka, orange juice and Galliano in roasting pan. Place duckling in pan and refrigerate for 6 hours. Turn several times and baste in liquid mixture. Dry bird and rub with garlic powder and cayenne pepper. Preheat the grill to 300°F. Cook duck on rack with water-filled drip pan below (ducks are quite fat and will render much fat). Cook for 30 minutes on each side or until cooked to internal temperature of 180°F. *Serves* 4.

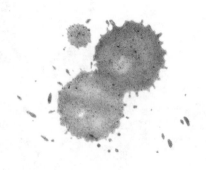

Soak wood chips or chunks in wine, beer, fruit juice or your favorite Scotch for at least an hour before using.

Ridgefield Smoked Duck

8 large duck legs

Dry rub:
½ teaspoon dried thyme
½ teaspoon salt
½ teaspoon freshly ground black pepper

Basting spray:
¼ cup cider vinegar
1 tablespoon barbecue sauce
Dash Tabasco sauce

Trim excess fat from legs. Rub thyme, salt and pepper mixture well into legs and marinate for 1 to 2 hours at room temperature in a covered dish.

Place the legs, skin side down, on smoker grill. Use fruitwoods or alder for smoke. Oak and hickory produce too strong a smoke flavor. Turn legs over after 1 hour.

Cook at 200°F for 2 to 21 hours until leg bone twists easily. Remove legs from heat and shred meat into a metal or ceramic bowl. Add vinegar, barbecue sauce and Tabasco and mix well.

Serve hot on thinly sliced toasted French or rye bread, lightly spread with garlic butter. *Serves* 4.

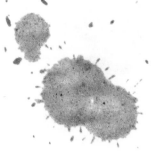

"Q" Birdies

4 Cornish game hens, $1\frac{1}{2}$ pounds each
Marinade:
1 cup tequila
1 cup Grand Marnier
$\frac{1}{4}$ cup olive oil
1 large sweet red onion, finely diced
$\frac{1}{4}$ cup cider vinegar
1 teaspoon paprika
$\frac{1}{2}$ teaspoon ground lemon pepper
$\frac{1}{4}$ teaspoon salt
$\frac{1}{4}$ teaspoon freshly ground black pepper
$\frac{1}{4}$ teaspoon garlic salt
Dash Tabasco sauce
Dash Worcestershire sauce

Wash and pat-dry hens. One day before you wish to barbecue, place birds in a 2-quart, sealable plastic bag. Pour in the marinade ingredients and place bag in the refrigerator. Chill for at least 12 hours, turning as often as convenient.

Before smoking, drain birds and save the marinade for basting. Let birds come to room temperature before putting in smoker. Place, breast side down, on grill and cook for 21 hours, basting every 20 minutes with the marinade. Turn at least two times during cooking. Birds are ready to serve when internal temperature reaches 180°F and legs move easily. Pierce one thigh with a fork; if the juices are clear, birds are done. Cover with foil and let cooked birds rest for 10 to 15 minutes. Serve whole or cut in half. *Serves* 4.

Meat thermometers take the guesswork out of barbecue, but they tend to become unreadable in a smoky grill. Use the instant-read variety. Keep them outside the oven and stick them in the meat periodically to check doneness. Their small probes do little damage to the meat.

Smok'n Chick'n

1 large chicken (5 pounds or more)

Marinade:
1 cup Italian salad dressing (the zestier the better)
$\frac{1}{2}$ cup spicy barbecue sauce
$\frac{1}{2}$ cup rice wine vinegar
$\frac{1}{2}$ cup apple cider

Dry rub:
$\frac{1}{4}$ teaspoon freshly ground black pepper
$\frac{1}{2}$ teaspoon paprika
$\frac{1}{2}$ teaspoon dried summer savory
$\frac{1}{2}$ teaspoon ground sage
$\frac{1}{4}$ teaspoon onion salt

Basting spray:
Apple juice

Wash and pat-dry chicken. Pour marinade into cavity and over chicken; sprinkle dry ingredients inside and over moistened chicken. Place in a sealable plastic bag. Marinate for at least 4 hours.

Place chicken in smoker and cook at 225°F for 4 hours, turning two or three times. Baste with apple juice several times. When done let bird rest sealed in aluminum foil for at least 20 minutes. Carve and serve with barbecue sauce on the side. *Serves* 4-6.

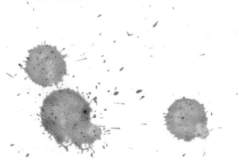

"Q" on the Wing

2 dozen chicken wings
$\frac{1}{4}$ cup lemon juice
$\frac{1}{4}$ cup vegetable oil
1 tablespoon salt
1 teaspoon garlic salt
2 teaspoons onion powder
1 teaspoon chopped cilantro
1 teaspoon paprika
1 teaspoon sugar
$\frac{1}{4}$ teaspoon ground ginger

Clip tips from wings. Mix lemon juice and vegetable oil. Sprinkle on chicken wings. Mix remaining ingredients. Roll chicken wings in resulting blend and refrigerate at least 4 hours. Cook wings until crisp. *Serves* 4-6.

Yellow Bird

$\frac{1}{4}$ cup lemon juice
$\frac{1}{4}$ cup corn oil
1 teaspoon mustard seeds
1 teaspoon onion powder
1 4- to 5-pound chicken, cut into pieces

Mix lemon juice, corn oil, mustard seeds, and onion powder. Turn chicken pieces in paste and place in a sealable plastic bag for 4 hours. Prepare grill to 250°F. Place chicken on grill and cook for 1 hour, turning often. *Serves* 4.

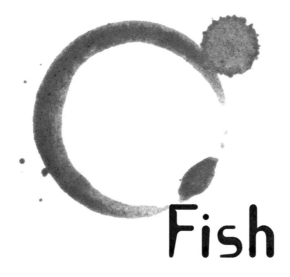

Fish

The Shell Game

2 dozen clams or mussels
1 tablespoon cornstarch
1 stick butter
Juice of 1 large lemon

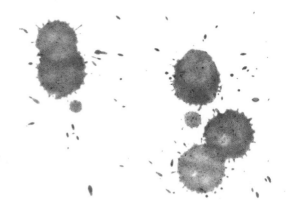

Scrub clams or mussels, cutting off any beard and discarding shellfish that are partially open. Mix cornstarch into a large pot of cold water. Place the clams or mussels in water-cornstarch mixture for 45 minutes. As they sit in the mixture, they will purify themselves. Prepare grill to high heat. When the clams or mussles are ready to come out of water-cornstarch mixture, rinse under fresh water. Place on grill and cover. Melt butter and stir in lemon juice. The clams or mussels will begin to cook in their own liquid and open in 5 to 10 minutes (check regularly). As they open (do not overcook), remove with tongs (the shells will be quite hot). Discard any that don't fully open. Remove meat with cocktail forks and dip in drawn butter or your favorite light barbecue sauce. Eat immediately if you are serving as snacks around the grill. If you are serving at the table, transfer open shellfish to container and keep in warm oven until ready to serve.

Clams and mussels aren't typically thought of as barbecue food, but if you think about it, an argument could be made that the clambakes of New England were some of the country's earliest "Q" events: the local bounty cooking over wood fires. At any rate, they make easy and quick grilling for those occasions when you don't have time to cook for the long haul. They also make great fill-in food when you're standing around the grill waiting for your big cut to finish. Clams and mussels adapt well to gas grill cooking as they cook quickly at fairly high temperatures. *Serves* 4.

One of the most treasured accolades in the "Q" world is the designation Ph.B. This Doctorate of Barbecue is sparingly awarded for "outstanding contributions to barbecue" by Remus Powers (the Dean of Greasehouse University) and the Kansas City Barbecue Society.

Jerry's Grilled Willapa Oysters

2 to 3 dozen large oysters

Marinade:
$\frac{1}{2}$ cup melted butter or margarine
$\frac{1}{2}$ cup white wine
$\frac{1}{4}$ cup sweet barbecue sauce
2 tablespoons lemon juice
1 tablespoon chopped garlic
1 tablespoon chopped fresh parsley
Dash Tabasco sauce

Mix butter, wine, barbecue sauce, lemon juice, garlic, parsley and Tabasco in a bowl and set aside.

Place unshucked oysters on a very hot grill and heat until oysters open. Using heat-proof barbecue gloves, carefully remove top shell and place oysters back on grill.

Drizzle marinade onto each oyster and close top of grill. Heat 4 to 5 minutes and serve hot from the grill. Have plenty of bread available to soak up oyster juice-sauce mixture. Good with wine, beer or Jack Daniel's (taken neat only). *Serves 4.*

As a special treat, two of the photographers at The Columbian invited me to dinner—a special dinner featuring seven dozen Willapa Bay oysters. They couldn't cook them quickly enough for their two guests and we all downed the shelled delicacies as fast as they came off the grill. Fresh, fresh oysters are the secret here.

Salmon Steaks à la Roger

4 large 1½-inch-thick salmon steaks

Marinade:
½ cup packed light brown sugar
¼ cup butter or margarine
¼ cup honey
¼ cup mango juice
1 tablespoon brandy
Dash crushed red pepper

Flavored butter:
2 tablespoons mashed mango
¼ teaspoon ground white pepper
¼ teaspoon dried dill
½ cup butter, softened

Combine marinade ingredients and cook in a saucepan for 4 to 5 minutes over low heat. Place salmon in glass baking dish and pour cooled marinade over steaks. Turn often as you marinate for 1 hour.

While fish is grilling, mix mashed mango, white pepper and dill with softened butter and set aside.

Brush off excess marinade and reserve to baste steaks during cooking. Grill over hot coals for approximately 12 minutes per side. Serve with 1 teaspoon of mango butter on the side or on top of steaks. *Serves* 4.

Salmon Martini

¼ cup fresh dill sprigs
1 teaspoon rock salt
1 teaspoon cracked black pepper
1 butterflied salmon (minus head and tail)
2 cups gin or vodka
½ cup dry vermouth (less for dry martini enthusiasts)
¼ cup olive oil
2 teaspoons dried thyme
1 bay leaf
2 teaspoons onion powder
2 teaspoons rock salt
Juice of 1 large lemon

Mix dill, salt and pepper and rub into exposed surface of fish. Place fish, covered, in refrigerator for 2 hours. Mix alcohol, vermouth, oil, thyme, bay leaf, onion powder, salt and lemon juice (shaking or stirring according to your mixological philosophy). Pour over fish and return to refrigerator for 3 hours. Prepare grill at 300°F using alder wood, if available. Reserve marinade and warm in a saucepan. Let salmon stand at room temperature for 30 minutes before cooking. Place salmon, exposed side down, on foil away from fire for 35 minutes. Turn and mop with reserved liquid. Cook for 35 minutes or until done.

High-octane cocktails are mercifully back in vogue and it seems only right to treat the condemned salmon to a final martini before putting it on the grill. *Serves* 4-6.

Lemon Grilled Catfish

½ cup unsalted butter, softened
1 garlic clove, crushed
6 catfish fillets, about 5 to 7 ounces each
2 tablespoons lemon pepper

Combine butter and garlic in a bowl; mix well.
Coat both sides of fillets lightly with some of
the butter mixture; sprinkle with lemon pep-
per. Place fillets on grill rack in covered grill.
Grill over medium-hot coals for 6 to 7 minutes.
Turn and baste with remaining butter mixture.
Grill for 5 minutes more or until fish flakes eas-
ily. Serve with barbecue or fruit salsa. *Serves 6.*

Carolyn Wells, Kansas City
Carolyn is the "Godmother" of barbecue and of this
book, and a true and dear friend.

Over the Rainbows

$\frac{1}{4}$ cup melted butter or margarine

1 tablespoon lime juice concentrate

4 large $1\frac{1}{2}$- to 2-pound rainbow trout
   (fresh, if possible), cleaned

$\frac{1}{4}$ cup finely crushed Kaffir lime leaves

$\frac{1}{4}$ cup packed light brown sugar

1 tablespoon freshly ground black pepper

$\frac{1}{2}$ teaspoon garlic salt

Cheesecloth soak:

$\frac{1}{2}$ cup olive oil

$\frac{1}{4}$ cup lime juice concentrate

1 tablespoon salt

Combine butter and lime juice concentrate and brush trout inside with this mixture. Roll in a mixture of lime leaves, sugar, pepper and salt, coating well. Tightly wrap each fish in cheesecloth and refrigerate overnight. Before smoking, bring fish to room temperature by setting on counter for 30 minutes.

Place whole wrapped fish in glass baking dish and pour the soak over each fish; let cheesecloth absorb the liquid. Place fish on grill and cook 40 to 50 minutes in 200°F smoker. If you can use alder, lime or lemon wood for smoke flavor, the results will be incredible. Otherwise, use a very light oak wood for approximately half the cooking time. DO NOT USE HICKORY.

Serve on a platter with fish still wrapped in cheesecloth. Cut them open at tableside for dramatic effect. *Serves* 4.

One really serious approach to "Q" utensils we've seen is one of those large tool chests on castors that car mechanics use. They lock up tight, can stow just about anything and move easily from garage to patio as the seasons change.

Dave's World Famous BBQ Basting Sauce

2 sticks (1 cup) butter
$\frac{1}{3}$ cup lemon juice
$1\frac{1}{2}$ teaspoons soy sauce
$1\frac{1}{2}$ teaspoons Worcestershire sauce
1 tablespoon chopped fresh parsley
1 teaspoon sweet basil
$\frac{1}{2}$ teaspoon garlic powder
Salt and pepper to taste

Melt the butter and add the remaining ingredients. Use to baste salmon, albacore or other firm fish while cooking. *Makes about $1\frac{1}{3}$ cups.*

Before grilling or smoking, use a nonstick cooking spray to coat the grill itself and the inside lid of the smoker or grill. Makes cleanup easier and food won't stick.

BQ Albacore

4 albacore tuna steaks, about $\frac{1}{2}$ to
  $\frac{3}{4}$ inch thick
8 strips bacon
2 cups soy sauce
1 tablespoon lemon juice
2 garlic cloves, finely chopped
Dash Tabasco sauce
Salt and pepper to taste

Wrap each albacore steak with 2 pieces of bacon and secure with a toothpick. Put steaks in a glass baking dish and marinate overnight in the soy sauce, lemon juice, garlic, Tabasco, salt and pepper mixture to which enough water has been added to cover fish. One hour before you wish to barbecue, let fish come to room temperature.

Barbecue off heat, adding hickory, alder or fruit wood chips to briquette side of barbecue. Cook 4 to 6 minutes per side until fish is done but still moist. *Serves 4.*

Cat Talbot, captain
Fishing Vessel Millie C,
Mendocino, California

Char-Broiled King Salmon Fillets

2 pounds fresh king salmon fillets
10 tablespoons unsalted butter, softened
3 tablespoons lime juice
1 shot tequila (use Cuervo for best taste)
1 ripe avocado
2 tablespoons chopped cilantro
2 tablespoons water
1 tablespoon olive oil
1 teaspoon chopped garlic
1 teaspoon chopped shallots
3 tablespoons chicken stock
Salt and pepper to taste

Prepare the barbecue grill. Cut the fillet into four portions, discarding bones. Cover and refrigerate. In a food processor, combine the butter, 1 tablespoon lime juice, and tequila. Process until smooth and set aside. In a bowl, mash the avocado with 1 tablespoon cilantro and the water; add salt to taste and set aside.

To prepare the sauce, heat a sauté pan, add the olive oil, and lightly sauté the garlic and shallots. Add the remaining 2 tablespoons lime juice, the mashed avocado, and the chicken stock; salt and pepper to taste and bring to a gentle boil.

When grill is hot, coat the salmon fillets with the tequila butter, salt and pepper, and grill on each side for 3 minutes per side. Transfer to a warm serving platter. Add the remaining 1 tablespoon of cilantro to the sauce, pour over the salmon, and serve. *Serves* 4.

Smoking should be done at between 200°F and 220°F. If the temperature gets too high, close the dampers; if temperature is too low, open them and add more soaked wood chips or wood chunks.

White Tie and Lobster Tails

1 stick butter, or as much as needed
1 teaspoon thyme
Juice of 1 lemon
Salt and pepper to taste
1 lobster per person

Melt butter and mix with thyme, lemon juice, salt and pepper. Keep over low heat. Plunge lobsters in large kettle of vigorously boiling water. When water comes to a second boil, remove now-dead lobsters with tongs, being very careful not to scald yourself. Wrap in towels to protect yourself from burning and snap off tails. Replace remainder of lobsters (or just the claws, if you don't like body meat) in boiling water and boil as you normally would lobster. With a stout knife, split lobster tail from end to end, cutting through soft underside first. Brush exposed meat with butter mixture. Place, shell side down, on grill over medium heat. Brush again in 20 minutes and turn over for 5 to 10 minutes. Serve with tails and bodies, using remainder of butter mixture for dipping.

As a New Englander, I used to be a snob about lobsters, saying: "Water is the only cooking medium for these noble warriors of the deep, and you mustn't ever smoke them." I had to travel to Hawaii, where I sampled the large, clawless variety, to get my head turned around on that one. I still believe that smoking the tender claws is overkill and shouldn't be done, but don't let anyone tell you the tails can't benefit from a whiff of smoke. If you're worried that lobsters are too expensive and high-falutin for your "Q" cronies, consider this: It has only been relatively recently that these crustaceans were considered the domain of the tuxedo crowd (mainly due to escalating prices). You only need to wrestle with shelling one of these babies to be disabused of the notion that they are for dainty company. Besides, when New England was first settled, lobsters were so plentiful that they were regularly served to prisoners in colonial jails.

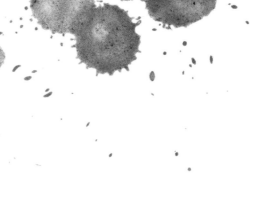

Dodie's Salmon Cream Sauce

2 cups whipping cream
2 egg yolks
$2\frac{1}{2}$ tablespoons mustard
$2\frac{1}{2}$ tablespoons flour
$\frac{1}{2}$ cup soft margarine
$\frac{1}{2}$ small onion, chopped
Juice of 1 lemon
Pinch tarragon
Pinch parsley

Blend ingredients in a bowl with a wire whisk, or in a blender. Place in a saucepan and cook over low heat until mixture thickens. Serve with salmon fillets or steaks. *Makes about $2\frac{1}{2}$ cups.*

Dodie Scott
Fishing Vessel Sabrina, Fort Bragg, California

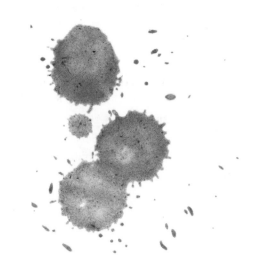

New Yorkers used to barbecue turtles in the early 18th century.

Rum Soused
BBQ Shrimps

2 pounds medium shrimp (about 32)

Lime and mango ratatouille:

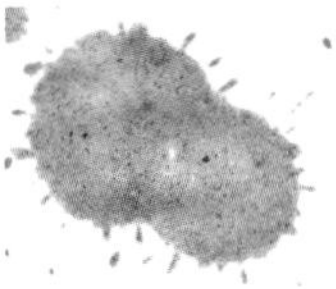

3 ripe mangos
1 green pepper
1 small sweet red onion
1 cup pineapple juice
$\frac{1}{4}$ cup lime juice
3 tablespoons balsamic vinegar
1 tablespoon chopped fresh basil
Freshly ground black pepper and salt to taste

Marinade:

$1\frac{1}{2}$ cups pineapple juice
$\frac{1}{2}$ cup light or dark rum
6 tablespoons fresh lime juice (4 limes)
2 tablespoons chopped fresh parsley
2 garlic cloves, minced
$\frac{1}{2}$ teaspoon sea salt
$\frac{1}{2}$ teaspoon freshly ground black pepper

Peel and finely dice mangos, carefully cutting fruit away from large pit. Seed and finely dice green pepper. Finely dice red onion. Mix fruit-vegetable mixture with liquid ingredients. Add chopped basil and pepper and salt, and stir. Set aside.

Combine marinade ingredients in a large bowl, add shrimp and refrigerate for 2 to 3 hours only. (More time than that will allow the citric acid in the marinade to begin to "cook" the shrimp.) Drain shrimp and put on grill in smoker (pre-heated to 200°F) for 15 to 20 minutes until they are just cooked through. Test one to see if it's done. Remove from grill and chill for several hours. Serve with the bowl of lime and mango ratatouille for dipping shrimp. *Serves* 4-6.

If you don't have an expensive thermometer on your rig, a candy thermometer mounted in a hole in the lid will do the trick. They measure in about the right heat range you will cook in and have a probe long enough to monitor the middle of the grill. In a pinch, put your palm over the grill top. If you can hold it there for five seconds, the fire is low enough for real barbecue.

Ol' Man Catfish

6 catfish fillets, 8 to 10 ounces each (fresh, if possible)

Dry marinade:
$\frac{1}{2}$ cup olive oil
$\frac{1}{2}$ cup rosé or blush wine
1 tablespoon finely diced shallots
2 teaspoons sea salt
2 teaspoons freshly ground white pepper
1 teaspoon onion powder
1 teaspoon brown sugar

Steaming liquid:
2 cups rosé or blush wine
4 cups water
2 lemons, thinly sliced

Rub fillets generously with the dry marinade and refrigerate overnight. Bring to room temperature just before cooking.

When smoker reaches 200°F, pour wine and water into water pan. Float lemon slices in the pan. Place fillets on grill over water pan and cook for 1 to 1$\frac{1}{2}$ hours, checking fish often. Fillets are ready when they flake and flesh is firm and opaque. Serve on a heated platter decorated with sliced lemons and kosher salt. *Serves 6.*

Kecap manis, a Malaysian sauce, evolved over the years to something we are all familiar with: ketchup.

Sauterne Smoked Shark

4 shark steaks, 8 to 10 ounces each

Marinade:

1 cup Sauterne wine
$\frac{1}{4}$ cup melted butter or margarine
$\frac{1}{4}$ cup extra virgin olive oil
1 tablespoon capers
2 or 3 garlic cloves, minced

Fish rub:

1 tablespoon freshly ground black pepper
1 tablespoon finely chopped lemon basil
$\frac{1}{2}$ teaspoon salt
$\frac{1}{4}$ teaspoon ground ginger

Combine marinade ingredients. Marinate shark steaks in a glass baking dish or in plastic bags. Best if left soaking in the refrigerator for 6 to 8 hours, but can be used more quickly, if necessary. Drain steaks and save marinade. Cook reserved liquid in a saucepan until it reaches a full boil.

Prepare smoker and adjust to 200°F. Generously sprinkle fish rub on both sides of steaks and place them on oiled grill.

Baste steaks twice during the 40-minute cooking period. Serve steaks on a metal platter, which you have heated on high in the oven. Steaks should sizzle when they are put on the platter. *Serves* 4.

When barbecuing delicate fish like salmon, don't be afraid to use foil on the grill and grease it with oil or cooking spray. It may offend hardened outdoors types, but it will save you a lot of grief in the long run. The fish won't stick to the grill, and you won't be pulling pieces out of the embers. It also makes for a much less odoriferous cleanup job.

Beef

Barbecued Brisket of Beef

1 10- to 12-pound beef brisket
  (packer trimmed)

Brisket rub:

$\frac{1}{2}$ cup paprika

$\frac{1}{4}$ cup black pepper

$\frac{1}{4}$ cup salt

$\frac{1}{4}$ cup turbinado sugar

3 tablespoons garlic powder

2 tablespoons chili powder

1 tablespoon onion powder

1 tablespoon dry mustard

1 tablespoon celery salt

$\frac{1}{2}$ teaspoon red pepper

Brisket spray:

1 cup apple cider vinegar

$\frac{1}{2}$ cup beer

1 tablespoon Worcestershire sauce

1 tablespoon olive oil

Fill flour or corn tortillas or gorditas with chopped BBQ pork shoulder or brisket for a tasty luncheon treat.

Combine rub ingredients and massage into brisket. Seal in a plastic bag and refrigerate overnight. Before you barbecue, remove brisket from refrigerator and let it sit at room temperature for 1 hour. Prepare water smoker and bring temperature to 220°F. Fill water pan with water and 16 ounces of beer. Cut one orange and one lemon into thin slices and float in pan.

Place brisket in center of grill over water pan, fat side up, and cook until done. Brisket will shrink dramatically and turn almost totally black. Cook 1 to $1\frac{1}{4}$ hours per pound, a minimum of 12 hours, basting every hour with spray bottle of vinegar, beer, Worcestershire sauce and olive oil mixture.

When cooked, remove meat from grill, spray one more time and seal in aluminum foil. Slice across the grain and serve with a favorite barbecue sauce on the side. *Serves 12-16.*

Rattlesnake Prime Rib

1 10- to 12-pound standing rib roast, preferably prime

Rib rub:
$\frac{1}{2}$ cup olive oil
$\frac{1}{4}$ cup coarsely ground black pepper
$\frac{1}{4}$ cup salt
$\frac{1}{4}$ cup garlic powder
$\frac{1}{4}$ cup brown sugar
1 teaspoon crushed red pepper

Steaming liquid:
2 cups red wine
4 cups water
4 rosemary sprigs
10 fresh basil leaves

Prime rib spray:
$\frac{1}{2}$ cup red wine vinegar
$\frac{1}{2}$ cup red wine
$\frac{1}{4}$ cup olive oil
2 teaspoons honey

Rub roast with olive oil, massaging it into the meat. Rub black pepper, salt, garlic powder, brown sugar and red pepper mixture into meat, coating all sides evenly. Cover tightly and refrigerate overnight. Before cooking, let meat stand at room temperature for 30 to 40 minutes. Heat water smoker to 220°F. Pour red wine into water pan with water. Float rosemary sprigs and fresh basil leaves in water. Place meat, fat side up, in center of grill and cook for $2\frac{1}{2}$ to 3 hours over oak, hickory or fruit woods. Spray every 30 minutes with rib spray. When internal temperature reaches 140°F, remove roast from smoker, seal in foil and let rest for 10 to 15 minutes. Carve and serve immediately. *Serves 8-10.*

Bodacious Brisket

1 4- to 6-pound beef brisket
$\frac{1}{2}$ cup paprika
2 tablespoons brown sugar
2 tablespoons chili pepper
2 tablespoons onion powder
$\frac{1}{4}$ cup yellow mustard
$\frac{1}{2}$ cup beer
$\frac{1}{2}$ cup apple juice

Trim fat from brisket. Mix paprika, sugar, chili pepper and onion powder. Spread mustard on brisket. Coat brisket with prepared rub. Prepare grill to 230°F. Cook brisket over indirect heat for 2 to 4 hours, turning every 30 minutes and spraying with a mixture of beer and apple juice. Brisket is done when internal temperature reaches 150°F. *Serves 6-8.*

A handy new item is the thermometer that has its readout outside the oven. You stick a probe in the meat, and a wire runs out to a digital counter that tells you the temperature without having to lift the grill lid. They even have alarms that tell you when the meat reaches the desired doneness.

Santa Maria Tri-Tip

1 3- to 4-pound tri-tip roast
4 garlic cloves, slivered

Tri-tip rub:
1 tablespoon rosemary leaves
1 tablespoon garlic powder
1 tablespoon salt

Tri-tip baste:
$\frac{1}{4}$ cup balsamic vinegar
$\frac{1}{4}$ cup olive oil
$\frac{1}{4}$ cup lemon juice
$\frac{1}{4}$ cup garlic powder
$\frac{1}{4}$ cup white wine

Combine the rub ingredients and work into the roast. Cover and refrigerate overnight.

Mix the basting ingredients and set aside. Let roast come to room temperature. Cut small slits in roast and stuff with garlic slivers. Place on grill away from coals; baste often, using rosemary branches as a brush. Cook 50 to 60 minutes for rare meat (140°F on meat thermometer and 150°F for medium).

Remove from heat and slice across the grain. Serve sliced on a plate or on French rolls buttered with garlic butter and grilled until toasted. *Serves 4-6.*

Smothered Smoked Steak

2 large flank steaks

Steak marinade/baste:
$1\frac{1}{2}$ cups tarragon vinegar
$1\frac{1}{2}$ cups hearty red wine
$\frac{1}{4}$ cup maple syrup
3 tablespoons Jamaican Pickapeppa Sauce
3 tablespoons steak sauce
2 tablespoons walnut oil
1 tablespoon ground ginger
1 tablespoon minced garlic
1 teaspoon salt

Combine all marinade ingredients in a large bowl. Pour half of marinade over steaks in a glass baking dish or roll steaks and place in sealable plastic bags. Refrigerate overnight, then bring to room temperature on countertop. Bring reserved marinade to a boil, then cook and refrigerate to use as a baste on steaks.

Remove steaks from refrigerator. Wipe off excess marinade. Throw remaining liquid away. Place steaks on grill in smoker, which has been preheated to 220°F. Cook for 35 to 40 minutes, using rosemary branches to frequently brush baste on meat. *Serves 6-8.*

Beef Short Ribs

$\frac{1}{4}$ cup Guldens mustard
$\frac{1}{4}$ cup olive oil
2 tablespoons lemon juice
2 tablespoons chopped fresh parsley
$\frac{1}{2}$ teaspoon garlic powder
$\frac{1}{2}$ teaspoon onion powder
$\frac{1}{2}$ teaspoon freshly ground black pepper
4 pounds beef short ribs

Mix mustard, oil, lemon juice, parsley, garlic powder, onion powder and pepper, beating thoroughly. Coat ribs with mixture. Cover and refrigerate 4 hours. Heat grill to 300°F. Let ribs stand at room temperature for 30 minutes. Wrap ribs loosely in aluminum foil. Grill for 2 hours or until ribs are tender. *Serves 4.*

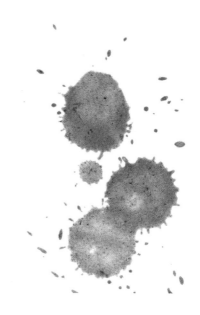

Kansas City Strip Steaks

$\frac{1}{4}$ cup Guldens mustard
2 tablespoons lime juice
1 tablespoon brown sugar
1 tablespoon prepared horseradish
2 teaspoons salt
$\frac{1}{2}$ teaspoon ground white pepper
4 Kansas City strip steaks, about 1 inch thick
   and 8 ounces each

Mix mustard, lime juice, brown sugar, horseradish, salt and pepper, turning it to a paste. Coat steaks. Marinate in a plastic bag in the refrigerator for 2 hours. Allow to stand at room temperature for 30 minutes. Grill steaks over low heat until done, turning once. *Serves 4.*

On our first trip to Kansas City, we were in a famous steak emporium called the Hereford House and asked what the Kansas City strip steak was on the menu. The waitress described it and we made the mistake of commenting that it sounded pretty much like New York strip steak. "How many steers," she asked, "have you ever seen in New York?" Touché!

Roast Beef

1 cup cooking sherry
1 cup vinegar
1 3-pound boneless rib roast, tied
Vegetable oil
Ground black pepper
Chopped fresh parsley
Dried rubbed sage
Dried rosemary
Dried thyme

The night before you cook, mix sherry and vinegar and pour into a plastic bag. Insert roast and tie shut. Refrigerate, turning occasionally. One hour before grilling, remove roast and pat-dry. Reserve liquid and boil for basting. Slather on vegetable oil and coat with pepper, parsley, sage, rosemary and thyme to taste. Prepare grill to 250°F. Place beef on grill away from fire with drip pan underneath. Cook for 11 hours (about 25 minutes per pound), basting regularly. Closely monitor internal temperature with thermometer. Cook to 10 degrees below desired doneness (130°F for rare, 140°F for medium, 150°F for well done). Remove and let stand until roast is done to desired temperature. Reserve drippings in pan for gravy. *Serves 4-6.*

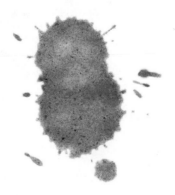

Sonny Bryan's flagship restaurant, The Original, is a nondescript building in a nondescript part of Dallas. Some of Sonny's regular customers include Arnold Swarzenegger, Steven Spielberg, Tom Hanks, former president George Bush, Sylvester Stallone, Eric Clapton, Larry Hagman, Bruce Willis, Jimmy Buffett and Donald Trump.

Foggy City
Meat Loaf

Loaf mop:

1 cup cider vinegar

$\frac{1}{2}$ cup hearty red wine

2 garlic cloves, roughly chopped

2 tablespoons olive oil

1 tablespoon dried summer savory

1 tablespoon Worcestershire sauce

Meat loaf:

1 medium onion, minced

1 medium red pepper, minced

$\frac{1}{2}$ cup sun-dried tomatoes,
   minced and freshened in warm water

2 tablespoons olive oil

$1\frac{1}{2}$ pounds ground beef
   (tri-tip or sirloin)

$\frac{1}{2}$ pound ground pork
   (shoulder or tenderloin)

$1\frac{1}{2}$ cups crushed Ritz or Waverly crackers

1 egg

$\frac{1}{4}$ cup hearty red wine

3 tablespoons favorite barbecue sauce

1 tablespoon minced garlic

1 teaspoon garlic salt

1 teaspoon lemon pepper

$\frac{1}{2}$ teaspoon dried oregano

$\frac{1}{2}$ teaspoon dried thyme

$\frac{1}{2}$ teaspoon dry mustard

Dash Tabasco sauce

Mix the loaf mop ingredients together and set aside. Preheat smoker to 220°F.

Sauté onion, red pepper, and sun-dried tomatoes until soft in olive oil in a heavy skillet. Place ground meat in a large bowl and add cooked vegetables and remaining ingredients. Using your hands, thoroughly mix into the meat.

Form meat into a loaf and place in a metal or glass loaf pan. Moisten the loaf with the mop and place in center of grill over water pan.

Cook for 1 hour without opening smoker. Then remove pan and remove meat in loaf shape and return to grill. Cook an additional $1\frac{1}{2}$ hours, mopping with liquid every 30 minutes. Ten minutes before you remove meat from heat, brush barbecue sauce or ketchup or a can of undiluted tomato soup on top of meat loaf.

Remove from grill, seal in foil and let meat rest for 10 to 15 minutes before serving. Slice in 1-inch-thick portions. Garnish with fresh parsley and serve a favorite barbecue sauce on the side. *Serves 4-6.*

Transplanted London Broil

¼ cup bourbon
1 London broil, about 2 pounds
Sugar
Salt
Ground black pepper
Mrs. Dash with garlic seasoning blend

Pour bourbon (flavor-rich small-batch brand, if you can afford it) into a small nonreactive pan. Place steak in pan and set in the refrigerator for 2 hours, turning frequently. Coat steak with sugar, salt, pepper and seasoning blend in that order. Reserve liquid for basting. Return steak to refrigerator for 1 hour. Prepare grill to 250°F. Place steak on high grill. Turn steak twice. Rotate twice. Cook 40 minutes or until done. *Serves 6.*

We think the inexpensive and unheralded London broil makes a great cut if you're planning to smoke steak. We've given it a drink of bourbon—America's true quaff—to make the transatlantic voyage a little easier.

Real Fajitas

1 tablespoon paprika
2 teaspoons freshly ground
   black pepper
1 teaspoon Tabasco sauce
1 teaspoon sugar
2 pounds skirt steak, trimmed
2 large green peppers
2 large red peppers
4 large onions
6 ounces pale ale
8 large tortillas

Mix paprika, pepper, Tabasco sauce and sugar and rub thoroughly into steak. Refrigerate for 3 hours. Slice peppers and onions. Prepare fire (preferably with mesquite) at 250°F. Lay beef and vegetables on grill, with vegetables as far away as possible from fire. After 30 minutes, turn beef and baste with ale. Remove vegetables. Sauté vegetables in oil until soft. Warm tortillas in the oven in aluminum foil. After 30 minutes, baste beef again and move over fire for searing. Drink remaining ale. Dice beef and peppers. Chop onions. Serve on tortillas with rice, refried beans, guacamole, and your favorite salsa. *Serves* 4.

While fajitas are now considered on menus across the country to be anything served with grilled vegetables in a tortilla, the word actually refers to a cut of steak. In Mexico, the skirt steak was slow-cooked to allow all of its flavor to express itself and then served in a taco. When the fajita became popular, the term was misconstrued to be the presentation and not the meat.

IncrEDIBLE Burgers

2 pounds ground beef

Beef seasoning:

3 tablespoons minced red onion

1 teaspoon garlic salt

1 teaspoon lemon pepper

1 tablespoon favorite barbecue sauce

1 egg, lightly beaten

1 tablespoon ginger ale

Steaming liquid:

16 ounces of your favorite beer

4 cups water

Burger spray:

1 cup apple cider

2 tablespoons balsamic vinegar

2 tablespoons olive oil

Mix meat and seasoning ingredients in a large bowl. Form into 8 patties, cover with plastic wrap and refrigerate for 1 hour. Remove meat from refrigerator and let it come to room temperature (approximately 20 minutes).

Preheat smoker to 220°F and pour beer and water into water tray. Add cuttings and skins from onions to the water. Place burgers on oiled grill. Cook burgers for 50 minutes, occasionally spraying with apple cider mixture. *Serves* 8.

Buzz's Barbecue Burgers

2 pounds fatty ground beef

1 medium onion, finely chopped

Paprika

Freshly ground black pepper

Garlic powder

Chopped cilantro

Ground cumin

Apple juice

Two hours before cooking, combine ground beef and onion in a bowl. Form into 8 patties. Sprinkle with paprika, black pepper, garlic powder, cilantro and cumin to taste. Bring smoker to 250°F. Place burgers on grill away from flame. Cook for 40 minutes or until cooked to desired doneness, occasionally spraying with apple juice. If cheeseburgers are desired, melt cheddar cheese over burgers 5 minutes before removing from grill. Serve on buns with mustard and ketchup or sauce of choice. *Serves 4-6.*

Some exotic woods to burn for flavorful smoke: lilac, seaweed, grapevines, fresh herbs (rosemary twigs), pieces of old wine or whiskey barrels.

Irish BBQ Flanque Steaque

¾ cup unsweetened applesauce
½ cup soy sauce
2 jiggers Bushmill's Irish whiskey, or to taste
3 tablespoons cider vinegar
5 garlic cloves
3 tablespoons chopped green onion
2 pounds flank steak
Spice Islands Beau Monde Seasoning
   (only while grilling the steak)

Mix applesauce, soy sauce, whiskey, vinegar, garlic and onion in a bowl. Puncture the meat all over with a fork and then place the steak in a plastic zip-lock bag and pour in the marinade. Leave meat in the refrigerator overnight, turning the bag occasionally.

Remove the flank steak from the marinade, scraping excess from the meat. Place the marinade in a medium pot and bring to a boil, continue heating until liquid is reduced by one-third.

Cook flank steak over hot coals until rare to medium rare. Slice the steak across the grain into thin strips. Arrange meat on plate and pour the reduced marinade sauce over the steak strips. *Serves 4-6.*

Skirt steaks, the diaphragm muscle of beef cattle, used to be called butcher steaks because they could hardly give them away. Now they sell well as the main ingredient in steak fajitas.

Flank Steak

1 flank steak, about 1½ pounds
1 cup Worcestershire sauce
¼ cup Tennessee whiskey
2 garlic cloves, minced
Olive oil
Freshly ground black pepper

The night before you grill, slightly score flank steak in a crisscross pattern on either side. Combine Worcestershire sauce, whiskey and garlic and pour over steak. Marinate in the refrigerator overnight, turning several times. Leave at room temperature for 1 hour before grilling. Prepare grill to high heat. Coat steak in olive oil. Grill steak quickly (3 to 5 minutes each side). Slice across grain into thin strips immediately after removing from grill. Pepper to taste. *Serves 6-8.*

Buffalo Steaks

¾ cup Italian salad dressing (the
  zestier the better)
2 tablespoons prepared salsa
1 tablespoon sugar
4 buffalo steaks, about 1 inch thick and 8
  ounces each
Salt and pepper to taste

At least 4 hours before cooking, combine dressing, salsa and sugar. Thoroughly slather steaks with marinade in a shallow nonreactive pan. Cover and refrigerate. Reserve excess for mopping. Prepare grill to low heat. Smoke for 1 hour or until meat reaches desired temperature (140°F for rare, 160°F for well done). Mop occasionally with remaining marinade. *Serves* 4.

Canadian entrepreneur Vern Jackson took to the barbecue circuit trying to drum up interest in smokin' with bison (American buffalo), which, he is fond of saying, "tastes like beef wishes it did." Low in cholesterol and fat, it may be a good choice for health-conscious carnivores. This is one way of cooking it.

Brisket Chili

1 4-pound beef brisket
Brisket rub (*page* 107)
1 cup chopped onions
2 garlic cloves, minced
1 green pepper, chopped
1½ tablespoons chili powder
1 teaspoon ground oregano
¾ teaspoon ground cumin
1 16-ounce can crushed tomatoes
1 16-ounce can kidney beans
½ teaspoon Tabasco sauce
½ teaspoon black pepper

Prepare brisket as Bodacious Brisket (*page* 107). Slice one quarter of meat into bite-size chunks. Serve remainder of beef immediately. In a large saucepan, place brisket chunks with onion, garlic and green pepper and cook over medium heat until soft. Add chili powder, oregano and cumin and cook for 3 minutes. Add tomatoes, kidney beans, Tabasco and black pepper. Cook over low heat for 4 hours. *Serves* 4.

HOURS OF OPERATION

MONDAY–FRIDAY 10AM–4PM
SATURDAY 10AM–3PM
SUNDAY 11AM–2PM
OR UNTIL THE FOOD RUNS OUT

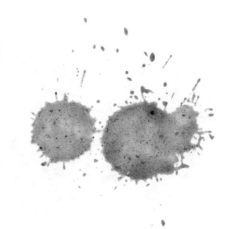

In smoked meats, as in poultry and fish, a pink color 3 to 1 inch deep under the outside surface is called a "smoke ring" and is one sign of great barbecue. Some barbecuers cheat by adding nitrates to their rubs, causing an unnatural smoke ring, but the proof is in the taste.

Side Dishes

Garlic Eggplant Grill

2 large purple or white eggplants
2 teaspoons seasoned salt
$1\frac{1}{2}$ cups olive oil infused with 3 blanched
   garlic cloves for 1 to 2 days
$\frac{1}{2}$ teaspoon Hungarian paprika
$\frac{1}{2}$ teaspoon freshly ground black or white pepper
Pinch ground nutmeg

Slice eggplants into $\frac{1}{2}$-inch slices (either hori-
zontal rounds or bowling pin-shaped length-
wise slices); sprinkle with salt on both sides
and lay in a colander. Wait 20 minutes to coax
out bitter liquid. Pat-dry with paper towels.

In a glass baking dish, drizzle oil and sprinkle
spices on each slice, then place slices, oil side
down, on hot grill that has been lightly coated
with vegetable spray. While cooking, drizzle oil
and sprinkle spices on other side. Grill 10 to 15
minutes, turning the slices occasionally until
they are tender, start to wilt and have some
charred edges. Serve piping hot. *Serves* 4-6.

If you cut an onion and only use
half and want to make the
remaining half last longer, rub
the cut surface with olive oil.

Bacon Corn Bread

4 slices smoked bacon
$1\frac{1}{2}$ cups stone-ground cornmeal
$\frac{1}{2}$ cup all-purpose flour
1 tablespoon baking powder
1 teaspoon baking soda
$\frac{3}{4}$ teaspoon salt
2 tablespoons sugar
2 tablespoons butter, melted
3 eggs, lightly beaten
1 cup buttermilk
1 cup corn kernels (preferably fresh)

Flavored butter:
$\frac{1}{4}$ pound (1 stick) butter, softened
2 teaspoons finely grated orange zest

Preheat oven to 400°F. In a well-seasoned cast-iron skillet, fry the bacon until crispy. Remove bacon, crumble and drain on paper towels. Save 1 tablespoon of the bacon grease.

Mix together the cornmeal, flour, baking powder, baking soda, salt and sugar. When well mixed, add melted butter, eggs and buttermilk and stir lightly. Add crumbled bacon and whole corn kernels.

Swirl bacon grease around bottom of skillet and coat sides using a small basting brush. Pour batter into skillet and bake for approximately 20 minutes. The top should be light brown with the edges darker. Serve in wedges with a dab of orange butter on the side of each serving. *Serves 6.*

Christopher Robert Dennis Browne, USC,
School of Cinema & Television
A chip off the old block. Must have picked up some talents from his Pa. Surprised us with this recipe one Labor Day weekend picnic. He had made both strawberry and orange butter. We all preferred the orange. Wow, he can cook too! Watch for his name at your local movie house.

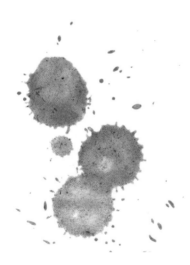

Smokin' Kebabs

4 red and green bell peppers, cut into
  1-inch squares
1 large eggplant, quartered and cut into
  1-inch cubes
4 Vidalia onions, cut into $\frac{1}{2}$-inch-thick wedges
12 cherry tomatoes
6 portobello mushrooms
1 large zucchini, cut into $\frac{1}{2}$-inch-thick rounds
$\frac{1}{4}$ cup corn oil
$\frac{1}{4}$ cup balsamic vinegar
6 large garlic cloves, minced
1 teaspoon dried basil
1 tablespoon chopped parsley
1 tablespoon chopped cilantro

Place all vegetables in a plastic bag. Mix oil, vinegar, garlic and herbs. Pour over contents of plastic bag. Refrigerate for 2 hours. Thread vegetables onto skewers, alternating types. Cook over medium heat for 20 to 30 minutes or until soft. Be particularly vigilant that tomatoes don't get too soft. *Serves 6.*

Grilled Tomato Soup

12 tomatoes, sliced OR
  6 tomatoes, sliced and
    1 6-ounce can tomato paste
$1\frac{1}{2}$ cups chicken broth
2 teaspoons chopped basil
2 teaspoons chopped parsley
1 teaspoon onion powder
$\frac{1}{4}$ teaspoon garlic powder
$\frac{1}{2}$ teaspoon freshly ground
  black pepper
$\frac{1}{2}$ teaspoon salt
2 tablespoons sugar
$\frac{1}{2}$ cup milk
1 tablespoon flour

Prepare the smoker for barbecuing at 180°F to 220°F, preferably burning hickory. Lay sliced tomatoes out on foil on grill and smoke for 30 to 45 minutes or until they brown slightly and start to wilt and curl up. Transfer directly to a large saucepan, trying to retain as much juice as possible. Over low heat, add chicken broth (preferably homemade from a bird you've smoked earlier) and tomato paste (if you choose method with fewer tomatoes). Allow to simmer for 15 minutes. Use wooden spoon to crush tomatoes and then transfer mixture to a blender or food processor to purée. Return mixture to saucepan on stove and add basil, parsley, onion powder, garlic powder, pepper, salt and sugar. Slowly stir in milk and flour. Don't rush the flour into the pan or you will end up with a clump of flour in your soup. Simmer for 2 hours, stirring occasionally. If you have squeamish guests and want the soup to seem like Campbell's, you can strain the seeds out, but then you lose some of the charm. *Serves* 4.

Mom's Summer Salad

1 #2 can small peas, drained (reserve liquid)

2 #2 cans French-style green beans, drained (reserve liquid)

1 large sweet onion, finely diced

1 medium green pepper, finely diced

1 cucumber, finely diced

5 stalks celery, finely diced

1 small jar pimientos

1 cup sugar

$\frac{3}{4}$ cup cider vinegar

$\frac{1}{2}$ cup olive or vegetable oil

$\frac{1}{2}$ teaspoon salt

$\frac{1}{4}$ teaspoon freshly ground black pepper

Place all vegetables in a large stainless steel or crockery bowl and mix lightly. Mix sugar, vinegar, oil, salt and pepper in a separate bowl and pour over vegetable mixture. If vegetables aren't covered, add reserved liquid from peas and beans. Refrigerate for approximately 1 hour and then serve. *Serves 6-8.*

Margaret Brooks, Patterson, Missouri
Margaret Brooks' son, Charlie, is a member of the
Aporkalypse Now barbecue team and regularly serves
this delightful salad at team parties and functions.

Barbecued Garlic

1 whole garlic head
Olive oil

Cut bottom off of garlic head. Coat with oil. Wrap in 2 layers of aluminum foil, loosely closed at the top. Cook over hot coals until soft, about 20 minutes. Remove contents with a knife and spread on toast or vegetables. *Serves 2-3.*

Maui Wowee Onions

4 large Maui or Walla Walla onions
1 tablespoon olive oil
1 tablespoon pineapple juice
1 teaspoon Worcestershire sauce
$\frac{1}{2}$ cup melted butter or margarine
$\frac{1}{4}$ teaspoon garlic salt
$\frac{1}{2}$ teaspoon freshly ground black pepper

Preheat oven to 350°F. Cut off root of onions—do not peel off brown skin—and carve a deep X across the bottoms. Place each onion on an 8-inch square piece of double-weight aluminum foil. Mix the rest of the ingredients in a bowl and ladle 1 to 2 tablespoons of mixture over each onion. Seal foil packets tightly and bake for 35 minutes or you can place packets on barbecue grill, away from direct flame or coals, for 45 minutes. Carefully open foil packets as steam can scald you. Serve whole and watch as your guests scoop out soft barbecued onion from inside the skins. *Serves 4.*

It takes 35 pounds of potatoes, 18 quarts of oysters, 40 pounds of roast pork and 5 gallons of baked beans to feed 100 people.

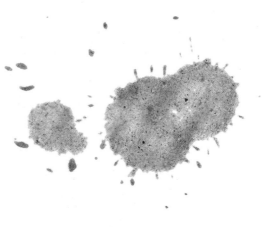

Uncle Grant's Sweet Taters

1 23-ounce can sweet potatoes, drained
(reserve liquid)
1 cup buttermilk
$1\frac{1}{2}$ cups packed brown sugar
2 eggs, beaten
$\frac{3}{4}$ teaspoon ground cinnamon
$\frac{1}{4}$ teaspoon ground nutmeg
$\frac{1}{8}$ teaspoon ground cloves
$\frac{1}{4}$ cup pear cider

Topping:
$\frac{1}{2}$ cup packed brown sugar
$\frac{1}{2}$ cup melted butter or margarine
1 cup chopped pecans or walnuts
$\frac{1}{2}$ cup Grape Nuts cereal
$\frac{1}{4}$ cup golden seedless raisins

Preheat oven to 325°F. Combine ingredients and pour into a well-buttered 8-inch square casserole. Bake for 40 minutes. While potatoes are cooking, mix topping ingredients. Pour over dish and return to oven for 15 minutes. *Serves 4.*

Grant Cline Lawson Browne,
Kimberly, British Columbia
Older brother of the author, Grant was chiefly responsible for guiding him through the backwoods and forests of Northern Ontario and instilling a love of Mother Nature, which lasts to this day. Plus he's a heck of a cook, especially on camping trips where he first mixed up these potatoes in a Dutch oven.

Kara Beth's Spud Salad

4 unpeeled baking potatoes
4 sweet pickles, finely chopped
6 green onions, finely chopped
4 hard-boiled eggs, shelled and chopped
Handful fresh mushrooms, sliced
1 teaspoon sugar
$\frac{1}{2}$ cup yellow mustard
$\frac{1}{2}$ cup mayonnaise
1 cup sweet pickle juice
Salt and pepper to taste

Preheat oven to 350°F. Bake potatoes in skins for 45 minutes.

Dice potatoes and put in a large bowl. Add remaining ingredients and mix well. Cover and place in the refrigerator until ready to serve. *Serves 4-6.*

Cranberry and Port Wine Chutney

12 ounces fresh cranberries
$\frac{1}{2}$ cup sugar
$\frac{1}{4}$ teaspoon ground cinnamon
1 cup port wine
3 tablespoons slivered crystallized ginger

The night before you plan to serve, wash cranberries and place in a pot with sugar, cinnamon and wine. Bring to a boil over high heat. Reduce heat and boil gently, uncovered, until cranberries begin to pop, about 5 minutes. Stir in ginger. Remove from heat and chill. Refrigerate overnight. Keeps for up to a week. *Makes about 2 cups.*

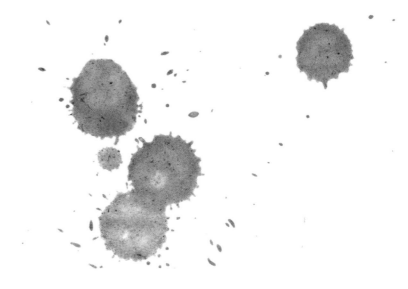

CB's Smokin' Taters

$1\frac{1}{2}$ pounds potatoes
2 large onions
1 cup ketchup
1 teaspoon Worcestershire sauce
$\frac{1}{2}$ cup olive oil
$\frac{1}{4}$ cup paprika
$\frac{1}{3}$ cup packed brown sugar
Drippings from 1 pound of bacon
   (crumble bacon and reserve)
Salt and pepper to taste
Fresh parsley, for garnish

Peel potatoes and onions and cut into quarters. Place in a large kettle, cover with water and add the remaining ingredients. Bring to a rolling boil, then lower heat and simmer for 35 to 40 minutes or until potatoes are soft. Drain, sprinkle with parsley and crumbled bacon and serve on a hot platter. *Serves* 4.

Stuffed Baked Potatoes

6 large potatoes
$\frac{1}{2}$ cup milk
$\frac{1}{2}$ cup shredded cheddar cheese
$\frac{1}{4}$ cup finely diced onion
Salt and pepper to taste

Wrap potatoes individually in aluminum foil and bake close to heat on grill for 45 minutes. Sauté onion until brown. Remove potatoes from grill, slice in half and remove most of contents from potato skins. Mix milk, cheddar cheese, onion and potatoes and mash together. Replace potato mixture in skins and wrap again in foil. Cook for 15 minutes more on grill. Add salt and pepper to taste. *Serves* 6.

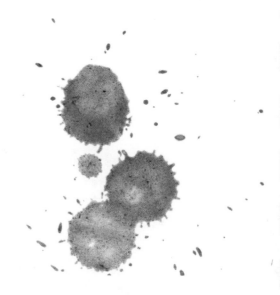

Rodney's BBQ Beans 'n' Bacon

6 slices smoked bacon, chopped
1 large onion, chopped into
   $\frac{1}{4}$-inch pieces
1 medium red or yellow bell pepper
1 16-ounce can pork and beans
1 16-ounce can butter beans
1 16-ounce can baked beans
$\frac{1}{4}$ cup packed brown sugar
$\frac{1}{4}$ cup blackstrap molasses
$\frac{1}{4}$ teaspoon garlic salt
$\frac{1}{2}$ teaspoon maple pepper
1 tablespoon balsamic vinegar
1 tablespoon prepared yellow mustard

Preheat oven to 350°F. Cook bacon until it begins to be transparent. Add chopped onion and red bell pepper and sauté until soft. Add the beans and the remaining ingredients. Cover and bake for 30 minutes. *Serves 8-10.*

Rod Patten, somewhere in his truck,
somewhere in America
A truck-drivin' man, Rod first introduced me to his special beans in Salt Lake City, Utah. They are best served with garlic bread and spicy barbecue brisket. He once entered them in a barbecue contest in Fort Worth, Texas, but didn't win. Too bad for the judges— they missed bean heaven!

Baked Pineapple

1 can pineapple chunks
1 tart apple, peeled, cored
   and sliced thinly
1 cup sugar
2 tablespoons flour
5 slices day-old bread,
   cut into cubes
6 tablespoons butter

Preheat oven to 350°F. Drain pineapple juice and place in a saucepan. Place pineapple chunks in a shallow buttered 1-quart casserole and layer with apple slices. Bring pineapple juice to a boil and whisk in the sugar and flour and cook approximately 1 minute until thickened. Pour over pineapple and apple mixture. Pile bread cubes on top of pineapple. In the same saucepan, melt the butter and drizzle over the cubes. Bake, uncovered, for 45 minutes or until well browned. Delicious as a side with pork dishes. *Serves 4.*

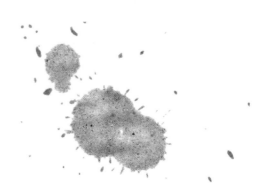

Desserts

Just Peachy Pie

1 cup sugar
2 tablespoons tapioca
1 teaspoon cinnamon
Pinch salt
1 teaspoon lemon juice
4 cups sliced peaches
2 plain pastry shells
2 tablespoons butter

Preheat oven to 425°F. Mix sugar, tapioca, cinnamon, salt and lemon juice with peaches. Let stand 15 minutes. Place in pastry shells. Dot with butter, cover and bake for 40 to 50 minutes. *Makes 2 pies.*

Magic Cookie Bars

2 sticks (1 cup) butter
1 cup graham cracker crumbs
1 14-ounce can sweetened condensed milk
1 6-ounce package semisweet
  chocolate chips
1 3-ounce package flaked coconut

Preheat oven to 350°F. Melt butter in a 13 x 9 inch pan. Sprinkle crumbs over butter. Pour condensed milk evenly over the crumbs. Top evenly with the remaining ingredients. Press down gently. Bake 25 to 30 minutes. *Makes 20 bars.*

Carolina 'nana Puddin'

4 cups whole milk
6 eggs
1$\frac{1}{4}$ cups sugar
$\frac{1}{8}$ teaspoon salt
1$\frac{1}{2}$ teaspoons vanilla or Grand Marnier
Dash ground nutmeg
1 box vanilla wafers
1 pint whipping cream
7 large, firm bananas (with a touch of green)

Scald milk by bringing to a boil, then immediately remove from heat. In the top of a double boiler, beat eggs, half of the sugar and the salt. Stir milk into the mixture and cook slowly over boiling water until custard starts to thicken (approximately 20 minutes). Remove from heat, add vanilla and nutmeg and set aside to cool.

Line a large pie plate or a 13 x 9-inch glass baking dish with vanilla wafers. Whip cream at high speed until it forms soft peaks, slowly adding the remaining sugar and set aside.

Slice the bananas into $\frac{1}{4}$-inch rounds and layer on top of the vanilla waffers. Spread approximately half of the custard over the bananas. Spread half of the whipped cream over the custard. Add another layer of vanilla wafers, another layer of bananas, the remaining custard and the remaining whipped cream.

Refrigerate for several hours. Serve individual portions of the pudding and dot each one with a banana round or two. *Serves* 10-12.

Ol' South Pralines

1 cup buttermilk
2 cups sugar
1 teaspoon baking soda
1$\frac{1}{2}$ cups pecan halves
1 teaspoon vanilla
1 teaspoon butter

Combine buttermilk, sugar and baking soda in a large saucepan and cook for 15 minutes, stirring constantly. Add pecans and cook until mixture reaches the soft ball stage. Remove from heat and let cook for 3 to 4 minutes. Add vanilla and butter. Beat until mixture cools and drop by spoonfuls onto lightly buttered wax paper. Serve when cool. *Makes about 3 dozen.*

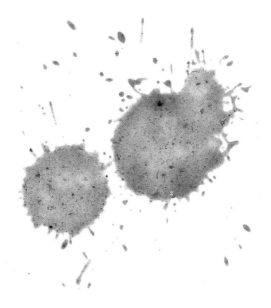

Grilled Stuffed Apples

4 large baking apples
$\frac{1}{2}$ cup raisins
$\frac{1}{4}$ cup currants
$\frac{1}{2}$ cup dry sherry or Marsala
2 tablespoons chopped walnuts or pecans
3 tablespoons brown sugar
2 tablespoons chopped maraschino cherries
1 tablespoon chopped dried apricots
   (soaked for 15 minutes in hot water)
$2\frac{1}{8}$ teaspoons ground cinnamon
$\frac{1}{8}$ teaspoon ground cloves
$\frac{1}{8}$ teaspoon ground nutmeg or allspice
3 tablespoons butter

Core apples, enlarging the hole with a grapefruit spoon or melon-ball tool. Place each apple on a sheet of heavy-duty aluminum foil. Mix the remaining ingredients except the butter in a large bowl. Spoon mixture generously into apples. Dot top of each apple with butter. Fold foil loosely and seal. Grill over low heat for 1 hour or until apples are done to your taste. Serve with vanilla ice cream (and caramel sauce, if you must). *Serves 4.*

Janeyce McCoy, Memphis, Tennessee
This recipe was entered in the Jack Daniel's Invitational Barbecue Contest dessert category and placed fifth in fruit entries. The Jack Daniel's is one of the only barbecue contests in the nation that has a dessert category.

Mom's American Apple Pie

Pie crust:
2 cups flour
1 teaspoon salt
$\frac{3}{4}$ cup shortening
5 tablespoons cold water

Pie filling:
$\frac{3}{4}$ cup granulated sugar
$\frac{1}{4}$ cup packed brown sugar
1 teaspoon ground cinnamon
6 to 8 cooking apples, peeled, cored and sliced
3 to 4 tablespoons butter

Preheat the oven to 350°F. Combine the flour with the salt and cut in the shortening until mixed. Add the water and mix with a fork. Shape into two equal balls and roll out. Combine sugars and cinnamon and toss with apple slices. Pour into pie shell. Dot with butter. Cover with top crust. Sprinkle with cinnamon sugar, if desired. Lay a piece of foil over the pie for the first 30 minutes to avoid browning too much. Bake for $1\frac{1}{2}$ hours. *Serves 6-8.*

Carol Frye, Reno, Nevada

Dorothy's Sweet Cherry Pie

3 cups pitted baking cherries
$1\frac{1}{2}$ cups sugar
$\frac{1}{3}$ cup flour
1 teaspoon vanilla
$\frac{1}{8}$ teaspoon salt
1 unbaked 9-inch pie crust and dough for
   lattice-top crust
$1\frac{1}{2}$ tablespoons butter
1 tablespoon kirsch

Preheat oven to 425°F. Mix cherries, sugar, flour, vanilla and salt and pour into unbaked pie crust. Dot with the butter and sprinkle with kirsch. Cover fruit with lattice-top crust. Brush with cold water and sprinkle with a little sugar. Place pie on a baking sheet or a piece of aluminum foil, to catch drips. Bake for 35 to 40 minutes until top crust is lightly browned. Serve warm with homemade vanilla ice cream. *Serves 6-8.*

Dorothy, Texarkana, Arkansas
Winner of many midnight diners' hearts and famed in local bake sales, Dorothy was a pastry cook at a tiny, hole-in-the-wall restaurant I discovered on a college trip in 1966. Late one night, after a barbecue dinner, I fell in love with her pie and begged her to give me the recipe. She refused but took my address. At Christmas that year I received a simple card and a handwritten copy of her treasure: her cherry pie recipe. Thanks Dorothy. You're in my heart and stomach forever.

If you don't have any buttermilk, you can make your own in a pinch. Just sour regular milk by adding and stirring a tablespoon of lemon juice or apple cider vinegar to a cup of milk.

JO-JA Peach Cobbler

5 cups sliced ripe peaches
1½ cups sugar
Pinch ground nutmeg
Pinch ground allspice
1 cup sifted flour
2 teaspoons baking powder
¼ teaspoon salt
1 stick (½ cup) butter, melted
1 cup milk

Preheat oven to 350°F. Butter a 13 x 9-inch glass baking dish, then lightly flour the bottom.

Cook peaches, ½ cup of the sugar, nutmeg and allspice in a saucepan over medium heat until soft, and set aside. Combine the remaining ingredients and whisk in the milk. Pour the mixture into the prepared baking dish, then carefully pour the softened peaches on top of batter. Bake for 40 to 45 minutes or until pastry is golden brown. Serve warm with fresh whipped cream to which you've added a dash of peach schnapps. *Serves* 10-12.

Barbecue judge's oath (delivered with all the seriousness of a church wedding, baptism or presidential inauguration):

"I solemnly swear to objectively and subjectively evaluate each barbecue meat that is presented to my eyes, my nose and my palate. I accept my duty so that truth, justice, excellence in barbecue and the American Way of Life may be strengthened and preserved forever."

Pineapple Upside-Down Cake

$\frac{1}{3}$ cup shortening
$\frac{1}{2}$ cup sugar
1 large egg
1 teaspoon vanilla
$1\frac{1}{4}$ cups flour
$1\frac{1}{4}$ teaspoons baking powder
$\frac{1}{2}$ teaspoon salt
Pinch ground nutmeg
$\frac{1}{2}$ cup reserved pineapple juice

Fruit topping:
2 tablespoons butter
$2\frac{1}{2}$ cups crushed pineapple
   (reserve liquid)
$\frac{1}{3}$ cup sugar
$\frac{1}{4}$ cup slivered almonds

Preheat the oven to 350°F. Cream shortening and sugar. When mixed, add egg and vanilla and beat until light and fluffy. Sift together dry ingredients, and add slowly to beaten mixture. Add the reserved pineapple juice.

In a 9-inch pie pan, melt the butter. Mix the pineapple, sugar and slivered almonds. Pour into pie pan. Spread cake batter over the topping. Bake for 45 to 50 minutes until bottom of cake is lightly browned. Remove cake from oven and let cool for 4 to 6 minutes, then carefully invert over serving plate and serve. *Serves 6-8.*

A pinch of baking soda mixed in with frosting made with confectioners' sugar keeps the frosting from hardening.

Spicy Oatmeal Cookies

1 cup shortening

1 cup sugar

1 cup honey

1 cup molasses

2 eggs

3 cups flour

1 teaspoon baking soda

2 teaspoons salt

1 tablespoon ground cinnamon

3 cups raisins

2 cups oatmeal

1 cup milk

1 cup nuts

Preheat oven to 375°F. Combine shortening, sugar, honey, molasses and eggs and mix well. Sift flour, baking soda, salt and cinnamon and stir into shortening mixture. Stir in raisins. Add oatmeal, milk and nuts. Dab onto cookie sheet and bake for 12 minutes. *Makes 7 to 8 dozen cookies.*

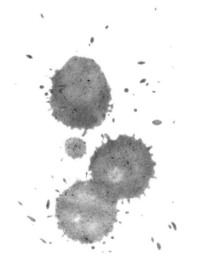

Tennessee Mudpie Cake

2 sticks (1 cup) butter

$\frac{1}{2}$ cup cocoa powder

2 cups sugar

$1\frac{1}{2}$ cups sifted flour

4 eggs, slightly beaten

$1\frac{1}{2}$ cups chopped pecans

1 teaspoon vanilla

Pinch salt

1 small bag miniature marshmallows

Frosting:

1 16-ounce box confectioners' sugar

$\frac{1}{2}$ cup half-and-half

$\frac{1}{3}$ cup cocoa powder

$\frac{1}{2}$ stick (4 tablespoons) butter

Confectioners' sugar, for garnish

Preheat oven to 350°F. Grease a 13 x 9-inch pan. Melt butter and add cocoa; stir well. Stir in sugar, flour, eggs, pecans, vanilla and salt and mix well. Pour mixture into prepared pan and bake for 30 to 40 minutes. While cake is baking, mix frosting ingredients and beat until smooth. Cover top of cake with miniature marshmallows while the cake is still warm and immediately spread the frosting over the marshmallows. Dust with confectioners' sugar. *Serves 10-12.*

Index